NOUVELLES
Histoires
drôles

39

Illustration de la couverture :
Philippe Germain

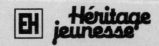

EH Héritage jeunesse

Nouvelles Histoires drôles n° 39
Illustration de la couverture : Philippe Germain
Conception graphique de la couverture : Michel Têtu
© Les éditions Héritage inc. 2001
Tous droits réservés

Dépôts légaux : 4e trimestre 2001
Bibliothèque nationale du Québec
Bibliothèque nationale du Canada

ISBN : 2-7625-1442-8
Imprimé au Canada

Les éditions Héritage inc.
300, rue Arran
Saint-Lambert (Québec) J4R 1K5
Téléphone : (514) 875-0327
Télécopieur : (450) 672-5448
Courriel : info@editionsheritage.com

*À tous ceux et celles
qui aiment collectionner,
écouter et raconter des blagues.*

— Bonjour! Je suis la gardienne.

— Bon, si Justin fait trop de bruit, s'il ne fait pas ses devoirs, s'il est désobéissant ou s'il te dérange, tu peux le punir en l'empêchant de regarder la télé et en l'envoyant se coucher plus tôt.

— Oui, mais s'il est tranquille et se comporte bien, qu'est-ce que je fais?

— Oh la la! Alors tu es mieux de prendre sa température!

* * *

La maman arrive à la maison et s'aperçoit que son fils a mangé tout le repas qu'elle avait laissé pour ses enfants.

— Mais voyons, Félix! Tu n'as pas pensé à ta sœur?

— Oh oui, j'y ai pensé! J'avais assez peur qu'elle arrive avant que j'aie fini!

* * *

À l'école, deux copines font leurs devoirs ensemble.

— Dis donc, Jessica, est-ce que ta calculatrice marche?

— Oui.

— Ah oui? Alors attache-la comme il faut!

* * *

Qu'est-ce qui est noir et rouge et qui vole?
Une mouche qui saigne du nez.

* * *

Papa nuage se promène avec son petit. Tout à coup, bébé nuage disparaît. Le papa s'inquiète et commence à chercher partout. Heureusement, il aperçoit son petit qui revient vers lui.

— J'ai eu peur que tu sois perdu! Mais où étais-tu donc passé?

— Je suis allé faire pluie-pluie.

* * *

— Papa, quand maman et toi vous serez en voyage, qu'est-ce que vous allez me rapporter en cadeau?

— Rapporter! Rapporter! Tu penses juste à recevoir! Une bonne fois, tu pourrais peut-être penser à donner!

— O.K. papa, quand vous reviendrez de voyage, qu'est-ce que vous allez me DONNER?

* * *

Natacha : Je peux jouer du piano sans me servir de mes mains.

David : Hein! Comment ça?

Natacha : Bien oui, je joue par oreille!

* * *

Chez le fleuriste, on lit sur une affiche : Dites-le avec des fleurs!

Bernard entre et commande une tulipe.

— Juste une? demande le fleuriste.

— Oui, je ne parle pas beaucoup...

* * *

Maman poule vient de pondre un bel œuf.

— Oh! s'exclame papa coq, il ressemble tellement à son frère au même âge!

* * *

Danielle et Jean-François courent à toute vitesse sur le trottoir :

— Ah non! On va encore être en retard à l'école!

— On serait mieux de se trouver une bonne excuse!

— Je le sais! On pourrait dire qu'en sortant de la maison, on a vu un vaisseau spatial atterrir, que des êtres en sont sortis et qu'ils nous ont emmenés avec eux faire un tour dans une autre galaxie!

— Eille! Le prof ne croira jamais ça!

— Tu trouves que c'est trop exagéré?

— Non, mais c'est ça que j'ai dit la dernière fois que j'ai été en retard!

* * *

Le prof : Votre garçon est très original!

Le père : Ah oui? Merci!

Le prof : Oui, il trouve chaque jour une nouvelle bêtise à faire!

* * *

Il était une fois un village où se trouvait une vieille maison abandonnée. Personne n'osait y entrer. Un jour, un garçon courageux décide d'aller voir ce qui se passe à l'intérieur.

Il ouvre la porte et entre, lentement. Il fait quelques pas et aperçoit un fantôme.

— Monsieur le fantôme, je crois que vous avez échappé votre mouchoir à côté de vous.

— Ce n'est pas mon mouchoir, c'est mon petit dernier!

* * *

— As-tu fait tes devoirs hier soir, Jean-François?

— Non.

— J'espère que tu as une bonne excuse.

— Oui, c'est à cause de mon père.

— Ton père t'a empêché de faire tes devoirs?

— Non, mais il ne m'a pas assez chicané pour que je les fasse.

* * *

— Mais maman! Pourquoi faut-il que je me lave les mains si je mange avec une fourchette et un couteau?

＊

Anne-Marie : Pourquoi les souris n'aiment pas les devinettes?

Ariane : Parce qu'elles ont peur de donner leur langue au chat!

＊

François est un grand sportif. Un jour sa maîtresse lui demande :

— François, dis-moi combien font trois et trois?

— Un match nul!

* * *

Cécile : Qu'y a-t-il de pire qu'une girafe qui a un mal de gorge?

Paul-Émile : Deux girafes qui ont mal à la gorge?

Cécile : Non, c'est un crocodile qui a mal aux dents!

* * *

Alain : Mes voisins forment un couple idéal.

Suzie : Qu'est-ce qui te fait dire ça?

Alain : Elle, elle est prof de mathématiques, et lui, il est plein de problèmes!

* * *

Sylviane emmène son ami visiter la vieille maison familiale.

— Alors, tu vois ici le lit où ont couché ma mère, ma grand-mère, mon arrière-grand-mère et mon arrière-arrière-grand-mère.

— Mon Dieu! Elles devaient être tassées!

* * *

L'élève : Saviez-vous que les enfants sont beaucoup plus intelligents que les adultes?

Le prof : Non, je ne le savais pas!

L'élève : Vous voyez ce que je veux dire!

* * *

La mère : Où t'en vas-tu comme ça?

Florence : Au magasin.

La mère : Avec ce chandail tout sale?

Florence : Non, non, maman, avec mon amie Vanessa...

* * *

À l'entrée du désert se trouve un dépanneur. Sur la porte, on peut lire : «N'oubliez pas d'acheter votre jus et votre eau en bouteille ici. Tous les dépanneurs que vous verrez dans le désert sont des mirages!»

* * *

Quel est le comble de la patience?
Tricoter des pantoufles à un mille-pattes!

* * *

Au bar laitier, un chien entre, s'assoit au comptoir et demande un lait fouetté aux fraises. Jean-Charles, qui était là, et la serveuse sont abasourdis. Le chien mange tranquillement son sundae et repart.

Jean-Charles : Je n'en reviens pas! C'est extraordinaire!

La serveuse : Je suis vraiment étonnée moi aussi! D'habitude il prend toujours un lait fouetté au chocolat.

* * *

— Que se passe-t-il avec ton chat et ton canari ces temps-ci? Il y a longtemps que tu ne m'en as parlé!

— Eh bien, imagine-toi donc que Mistigri a complètement cessé de courir après Pinson.

— Ah bon! tu as réussi à le dresser?

— Non, il a réussi à l'attraper!

* * *

— Sais-tu quel animal peut sauter plus haut qu'une maison?

— Non.

— Tous, voyons! As-tu déjà vu une maison sauter?

* * *

— La mère de Simon a trois enfants. Un s'appelle Tic, et l'autre Tac. Comment s'appelle le troisième?

— Toc?

— Non, Simon!

* * *

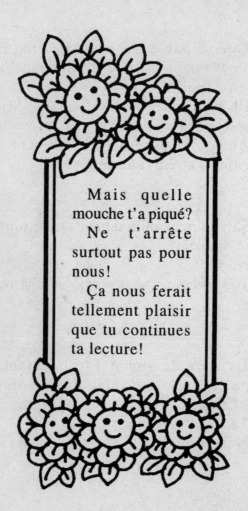

Mais quelle mouche t'a piqué? Ne t'arrête surtout pas pour nous!

Ça nous ferait tellement plaisir que tu continues ta lecture!

C'est le retour à l'école après les grandes vacances.

La prof : Et toi, ma belle, tu as passé de belles vacances?

L'élève : Oh oui! C'était fantastique... tastique... tastique!

La prof : Où es-tu allée?

L'élève : Eh bien, je suis allée visiter les Rocheuses... Rocheuses... Rocheuses.

La prof : Dis donc, il devait y avoir beaucoup d'écho!

L'élève : Oui! Comment as-tu deviné... viné... viné?

* * *

— Quel est le comble pour une chauve-souris?

— Je ne sais pas.

— Prendre rendez-vous chez le coiffeur!

* * *

Deux gros ballons se promenaient dans le désert. Soudain, un ballon dit à l'autre :

— Attention! Un cactussssssss...!

* * *

Deux nigauds se promènent en voiture. En descendant une grosse côte, celui qui conduit se rend compte que les freins ne fonctionnent plus.

— Hiiii! Il n'y a plus de freins! C'est la catastrophe!

— Mais non, ne t'inquiète pas! Je passe souvent ici, il y a un stop en bas de la côte.

* * *

Le père : Quel bulletin! Tu es le dernier élève sur 20.

Jocelyn : Oh, ça pourrait être pire, tu sais!

Le père : Comment ça?

Jocelyn : Je pourrais être dans une classe de 30...

* * *

Comment fait-on pour entrer un éléphant dans le frigo en quatre étapes?

On ouvre la porte, on enlève le pot de confitures, on pousse l'éléphant à l'intérieur et on ferme la porte.

* * *

Comment fait-on pour entrer une girafe dans le frigo en quatre étapes? On ouvre la porte, on sort l'éléphant, on place la girafe et on ferme la porte!

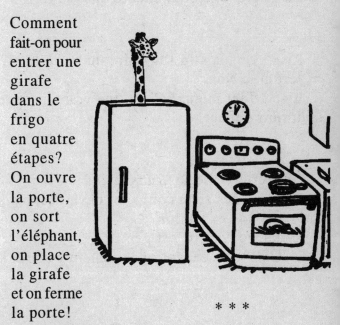

* * *

Le lion, le roi de la jungle, avait ordonné qu'un animal de chaque espèce participe au grand défilé qui aurait lieu le jour de ses funérailles. Quand le triste événement est arrivé, il ne manquait qu'un seul animal. Lequel?

La girafe, elle était encore dans le frigo!

* * *

Lise : Connais-tu l'histoire du lit vertical?
Jérôme : Non.
Lise : Tant mieux! C'est une vraie histoire à dormir debout!

* * *

Un frère et une sœur discutent :
— Il y a des sœurs qui sont bavardes, mais toi tu es une exception.
— Tu trouves? C'est gentil!
— Oui, tu es exceptionnellement bavarde!

* * *

Dans un petit café :

— Bonjour monsieur, dit la serveuse, que désirez-vous?

— Je voudrais une soupe, pas trop chaude, des légumes, pas trop cuits, une tranche de jambon, pas trop salé, et un petit café, pas trop fort.

— Et avec ça, aimeriez-vous un petit verre d'eau, pas trop mouillée?

***

Deux copains discutent :

— Salut vieux! Tu as bien l'air fatigué?

— Ah... si tu savais.

— Que se passe-t-il?

— C'est rendu que je ronfle tellement fort que je me réveille moi-même!

— Mais pauvre vieux! J'ai une solution toute simple pour toi.

— Laquelle?

— Tu n'as qu'à dormir dans une autre chambre!

* * *

Monsieur et Madame Thomie ont le plaisir de vous annoncer la naissance de leur fille Lana.

* * *

Ève : Qu'est-ce qui vole mais n'a pas d'ailes?

Jeanne : Je ne sais pas.

Ève : Un bandit!

* * *

La saison de la chasse au canard n'est pas encore commencée mais monsieur Galland y va quand même. Il est vraiment très chanceux car à peine deux heures après son arrivée, il tire sur son premier canard.

Il s'installe au bord d'un lac et commence à plumer sa prise. Soudain, il entend des pas. Comme il a très peur de se faire prendre par un garde-chasse, il lance l'oiseau au bout de ses bras dans le lac, et se met à siffler comme si de rien n'était.

— Bonjour monsieur! lui dit le garde-chasse.

— Bonjour!

— Je dois vous arrêter car la chasse au canard est interdite.

— Oui, oui, je le sais! Je ne chassais pas!

— Ah! non? Et c'est quoi, ce petit tas de plumes à vos pieds?

— Ça? C'est un canard qui est parti se baigner et qui m'a demandé de surveiller ses vêtements...

* * *

Un homme est penché par-dessus le garde-fou du pont Jacques-Cartier. Un policier l'aperçoit et s'approche de lui.

— Monsieur, avez-vous un problème?

— Oui, j'ai perdu mes lunettes dans la rivière des Prairies.

— Mais monsieur, ici c'est le fleuve Saint-Laurent!

— Oh! Moi, sans mes lunettes, je ne vois rien!

* * *

Un homme loue une chambre à l'hôtel. À minuit, il se fait réveiller par une voix qui dit :

— Je suis le fantôme à l'œil blanc!

L'homme a tellement peur qu'il se jette en bas par la fenêtre. Le lendemain, un autre homme loue cette chambre à l'hôtel. Lui aussi entend, à minuit :

— Je suis le fantôme à l'œil blanc!

Mort de peur, il se jette par la fenêtre! Le jour suivant, un troisième homme se présente et se retrouve dans la chambre. À minuit, encore :

— Je suis le fantôme à l'œil blanc!

— Ah oui? Eh bien! tais-toi sinon tu vas devenir le fantôme à l'œil noir!

* * *

La prof : Charlotte, le devoir que tu m'as remis sur ton chat Figaro est absolument identique à celui de ta sœur!

Charlotte : C'est normal, mademoiselle, nous avons le même chat...

* * *

Trois copains, Personne, Rien et Fou, se promènent en forêt. Tout à coup, Personne tombe dans un piège à loups! Rien se précipite vers son ami et demande à Fou d'aller chercher du secours. Fou court à toute vitesse vers son camion pour appeler le garde-chasse.

— Allô? Venez vite! J'appelle pour Rien, Personne est tombé dans un piège!

— Quoi? Êtes-vous fou?

— Oui, vous me connaissez?

* * *

Comment voyagent les abeilles pour aller à l'école?

En autobizzzzzzz!

* * *

Superman rencontre son ami l'homme invisible et lui dit :

— Salut! Je suis content de ne pas te voir!

* * *

— Sais-tu ce qui est pire que de manger une pomme et d'y trouver un ver?

— Non.

— C'est de manger une pomme et y trouver une moitié de ver...

* * *

— Sais-tu quelle est la pièce la plus violente de la maison?

— Non.

— C'est la cuisine.

— Pourquoi?

— Parce que c'est là qu'on bat les œufs, qu'on tranche le pain, qu'on pulvérise les noix, qu'on écrase les fraises et qu'on fouette la crème!

* * *

— Je ne veux plus aller à l'école. Personne ne m'aime. Les élèves me détestent et les profs aussi. Je veux rester ici, maman!

— Pas question mon grand! Écoute, dans la vie, il faut faire des efforts. Je suis sûre que tu as plein de choses à apprendre à l'école. Et puis, tu n'as pas vraiment le choix, c'est toi le directeur!

* * *

Deux nigauds discutent :
— Vois-tu la forêt là-bas?
— Non, les arbres me cachent la vue.

* * *

Guillaume : Fido, assis! Assis, j'ai dit! Ah! reste donc debout, espèce d'imbécile!

Évelyne : Franchement, ton chien aurait vraiment besoin d'aller dans une école d'obéissance.

Guillaume : J'ai essayé de l'emmener, mais il refuse d'y aller!

* * *

Lucie : Sais-tu qui a inventé l'école?

Diane : Oui, je crois que c'est Charlemagne.

Lucie : Toute une invention!

Diane : Ah! Que veux-tu... l'erreur est humaine!

* * *

Une petite fille est en compagnie de sa mère.
— Nous sommes deux! dit la petite fille.
Son père les rejoint.

— Nous sommes quatre! dit la petite fille.
Comment peut-elle dire ça?
La petite fille ne sait pas compter!

* * *

La mère : À qui as-tu parlé pendant une heure sur le balcon?

Sarah : À mon amie Jenny.

La mère : Mais pourquoi tu ne l'as pas fait entrer?

Sarah : Elle n'avait pas le temps.

* * *

— Que font les scorpions quand il pleut?

— Je ne sais pas.

— Ils se font mouiller!

* * *

Carole : Qu'est-ce qui fait zzib! zzib!

Thomas : Aucune idée!

Carole : Une abeille qui vole à reculons!

* * *

— Est-ce que tu crois aux girafes?

— Non, c'est un cou monté!

* * *

Rosange vient de passer une semaine au camp de vacances avec sa cousine. Quand vient le moment de se quitter, sa cousine lui dit :

— En arrivant chez nous, je t'écris tout de suite, sans faute!

— Oh, fais comme d'habitude, je finis toujours par comprendre!

* * *

— Qu'est-ce qui a un dos mais pas de ventre, a des feuilles mais n'est pas un arbre, a une couverture mais n'est pas un lit?

— Je ne sais pas.

— Un livre!

* * *

Comment s'appelle la plus grande cliente des magasins d'électronique?

L M H T O P I D T V !

* * *

Peter : Ma sœur vient de commencer un nouveau passe-temps.

Jules : Qu'est-ce que c'est?

Peter : Elle fait une collection.

Jules : De quoi?

Peter : Elle collectionne les puces.

Jules : Ah bon! Et toi, qu'est-ce que tu fais?

Peter : Moi, je me gratte...

* * *

La mère : Juliette, as-tu fini ta soupe à l'alphabet?

Juliette : Non, pas encore, maman. Je suis juste rendue à la lettre P.

* * *

Gabriel : Sais-tu quelle est la différence entre un citron, une roche et toi?

Jonathan : Non.

Gabriel : Le citron est sur, la roche est dure et toi c'est sûr que tu fais dur!

* * *

Samuel entre à la pharmacie et demande :
— Avez-vous des lunettes?

— Pour le soleil?
— Non, pour moi.

* * *

— Les élèves de ma classe m'appellent tous
Blé-d'Inde.
— Pourquoi?
— Je pense qu'ils maïs!

* * *

Un savant pose une puce sur son bureau et lui dit : «Saute!» La petite puce saute. Il lui coupe les pattes et lui dit encore : «Saute!» Mais la puce ne bouge pas. Il écrit alors dans son rapport : L'expérience démontre que lorsqu'on coupe les pattes à une puce, elle devient sourde.

* * *

Monsieur Chose : Je te promets, chérie, que je ne jouerai plus jamais à l'argent.
Madame Chose : Je ne te crois pas.
Monsieur Chose : Ah non! Combien tu gages?

* * *

L'explorateur : Dites-moi, quel est votre plat préféré?
Le cannibale : Les gens bons!

* * *

Le prof : Les élèves, je ramasse les devoirs.

Albert (tout bas) : Merci, Gabriel, de m'avoir laissé copier ton devoir. Un autre devoir manqué et le prof me coulait!

Gabriel : Ouais, je n'aime pas bien ça. J'espère au moins que tu n'as pas tout copié mot à mot?

Albert : Tu peux être sûr que oui! J'ai tout copié à la perfection! Et quand je dis tout, c'est tout!

Le prof : Albert, comment ça se fait que je n'ai pas ton devoir mais que j'en ai deux au nom de Gabriel Desroches?

* * *

Maman Poisson et papa Poisson se promènent en mer avec leurs petits. Ils croisent un sous-marin.

— Maman, qu'est-ce que c'est? demande un des petits.

— Ça, ce sont des hommes en conserve.

* * *

Duncan prend des cours de français. Il entend son professeur dire à un élève :

— Mon cher, tu es vachement avancé dans tes devoirs!

Duncan retient cette expression et s'en retourne chez lui. Il rencontre une jeune fille qu'il trouve pas mal jolie. Il prend son courage à deux mains et décide de lui parler un peu pour lui faire un compliment.

— Bonjour, je voulais te dire...

Comme il est très gêné, plus rien ne sort. Il a tout oublié ce qu'il connaît de français. En se concentrant comme il faut, la fameuse phrase du professeur lui revient!

— Bonjour, recommence-t-il, je voulais te dire que je te trouve jolie comme une vache!

* * *

Lise : Quelle est l'épice préférée des dentistes?
François : Je ne sais pas.
Lise : Le cari.

* * *

La fille : Maman, j'ai absolument besoin d'un dollar.

La mère : Pourquoi?

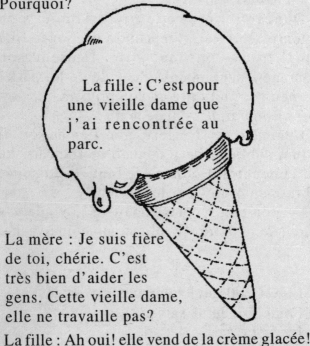

La fille : C'est pour une vieille dame que j'ai rencontrée au parc.

La mère : Je suis fière de toi, chérie. C'est très bien d'aider les gens. Cette vieille dame, elle ne travaille pas?

La fille : Ah oui! elle vend de la crème glacée!

* * *

Un nigaud invite son copain à la maison.

— J'ai quelque chose à te montrer.

— Oui, quoi donc?

— Eh bien regarde ce merveilleux casse-tête que je viens juste de terminer!

— Wow! c'est vrai qu'il est beau! Combien de temps as-tu mis à le faire?

— Six mois.

— Six mois! Franchement, c'est beaucoup!

— Un instant! Sur la boîte c'était écrit «4 à 6 ans»!

* * *

Deux copines discutent :

— Cette année, mes parents nous envoient, mon frère et moi, passer une semaine dans un camp d'été.

— Ah bon!

— Ils ont vraiment besoin de vacances!

* * *

— Regarde, j'ai trouvé un livre intéressant. Il parle des gens qui remettent toujours les choses à faire à plus tard. Tu devrais le lire!

— O.K., je te promets que je vais le lire... demain!

* * *

— Sais-tu quelle est la première chose que font deux crabes qui se rencontrent?

— Non.

— Ils se serrent la pince!

* * *

Drrring!

— Allô!

— Je voudrais parler à Claudine, s'il vous plaît.

— Il n'y a pas de Claudine ici. Je crois que vous vous êtes trompé. Êtes-vous sûr d'avoir composé le bon numéro?

— Absolument certain. Et vous, êtes-vous sûr que vous êtes dans la bonne maison?

* * *

— Sais-tu ce que ça fait un chat?
— Oui, ça miaule.
— Un mouton?
— Oui, ça bêle.
— Et une fourmi?
— Une fourmi? Non.
— Ça crohonde.
— Hein, comment ça?
— Eh oui, la fourmi crohonde!

* * *

— As-tu entendu la blague sur le plafond?
— Il est bien haut au-dessus de ta tête.

* * *

Depuis une demi-heure, Karine chante pour son amie.
— Tu aimes la belle musique? lui demande-t-elle.
— Oui, mais ce n'est pas grave, tu peux continuer à chanter quand même!

* * *

La mère : Qui a brisé cette vitre?
Louise : C'est Simon, maman. Il s'est

baissé juste au moment où je lui lançais une
boule de neige...

* * *

Gaston : Mais qu'est-ce que c'est que toutes ces bouteilles vides dans ton réfrigérateur?

Juliette : Ça? C'est pour mes invités qui ne boivent pas!

* * *

Didier : Maman! Je suis tombé dans un gros trou d'eau!

La mère : Ah non! Pas avec ton uniforme du collège?

Didier : Ben... je n'ai pas eu le temps de l'enlever!

* * *

— Pourquoi les humains lèvent un pied après l'autre quand ils marchent?

— Parce que s'ils levaient les deux en même temps, ils tomberaient!

* * *

Monsieur Jutras va visiter son voisin, monsieur Saint-Jean.

— Bonjour! Quoi de neuf?

— Eh bien, j'ai un chien maintenant.

— Où est-il?

— Juste là, à côté de la tondeuse.

Monsieur Jutras s'avance pour flatter le bel animal doré mais aussitôt qu'il s'approche, le chien lui saute dessus et l'attaque sauvagement.

D'une toute petite voix, monsieur Jutras dit à son voisin :

— Il est donc bien agressif! Où l'as-tu pris ton chien?

— Ah, c'est mon cousin qui vit en Afrique qui me l'a envoyé. Quand je l'ai eu, il faisait pas mal dur avec son paquet de poils longs autour de la tête. Mais j'ai tout coupé ça!

* * *

Quel est le comble pour un coq?

Avoir la chair de poule!

* * *

François demande à son grand frère :

— Qu'est-ce que tu as trouvé le plus dur quand tu as commencé à jouer au hockey?

— La glace!

* * *

Je suis un nez qui noircit des pages.
Un nez-crivain.

* * *

Trois gars s'en allaient en expédition dans le désert.

— J'apporte une gourde pleine d'eau, dit le premier.

— Moi, dit le deuxième, j'ai un parasol.

— Et moi, dit le troisième, je vais apporter une portière d'auto.

— Pourquoi? C'est lourd!

— Si j'ai chaud, je vais pouvoir ouvrir la fenêtre!

* * *

Le voisin :
Votre
chien a
encore
jappé toute
la nuit!
Savez-
vous que
c'est un
signe de
mort?

L'autre
voisin :
Non je ne
savais pas.
La mort de
qui?
Le voisin :
De votre
chien, s'il
recommence
une autre
nuit!

* * *

Deux copines discutent :
— Sais-tu qui habitait à côté de chez nous
quand j'étais petite?
— Non, qui?
— Mon voisin!

Un policier arrête une voiture et dit au conducteur :

— Bravo, monsieur! Vous êtes la millionième auto à traverser ce pont. Vous gagnez cinq cents dollars!

— Merci beaucoup! dit l'homme au volant. Ça tombe bien, je vais justement pouvoir me payer des cours de conduite!

— Pardon? dit le policier.

— Ne l'écoutez pas! dit la femme du conducteur. Il dit n'importe quoi quand il est soûl!

— Hein? s'étouffe le policier.

— Je le savais! dit le passager arrière. Je vous l'avais bien dit qu'on n'irait pas loin avec une voiture volée!

* * *

— Pourquoi les cultivateurs ont toujours l'air plus jeunes que leur âge?

— Parce que quand on sème on a toujours 20 ans!

* * *

Alexandra téléphone à l'épicerie :

— Bonjour, avez-vous des biscuits secs?

— Oui.

— Vous ne pensez pas qu'il serait temps de les arroser?

* * *

Au magasin :

— Je cherche un portefeuille imperméable.

— Mais pourquoi? demande la vendeuse.

— C'est pour mettre de l'argent liquide!

* * *

Que dit l'escargot sur le dos d'une tortue?

— Yahou!

* * *

— Quel est le nom de l'ex-champion de ski russe?

— Je ne sais pas.

— Ispet Lafiolenski.

* * *

— Sais-tu ce que la grande aiguille dit à la petite?
— Non.
— Rendez-vous à neuf heures moins quart!

* * *

Deux vers se rencontrent dans une pomme.
— Tiens! vous habitez dans le quartier?

* * *

La prof : Où es-tu né, Rodrigo?
Rodrigo : Je suis né en Amérique centrale.
La prof : Oui, mais quelle partie?
Rodrigo : Comment, quelle partie? Je suis né au complet en Amérique centrale!

* * *

Le père : Mange tes légumes!

Nicholas : Non!

Le père : J'ai dit mange tes légumes!

Nicholas : Non, bon!

Le père : Tu es mieux de manger tes légumes si tu veux devenir beau et fort!

Nicholas : Dans ce cas-là, papa, c'est toi qui devrais peut-être les manger!

* * *

Paul s'en va à son cours de musique. Il doit prendre un escalier de douze marches. Il en monte huit. Combien en reste-t-il?

— Quatre?

— Non, il en reste toujours douze!

* * *

Quelle est la différence entre ton petit frère et un biscuit?

Tu ne peux pas tremper ton petit frère dans un verre de lait!

* * *

Roberto s'en va au dépanneur :

— Avez-vous de la crème glacée aux cornichons?

— Non.

Roberto revient plusieurs jours de suite, mais toujours sans succès. Le propriétaire est bien désolé de ne pouvoir satisfaire son client. Il décide d'en commander, même si c'est très rare et très cher.

Roberto vient faire son tour au dépanneur :

— Avez-vous de la crème glacée aux cornichons?

— Oui, tu vas être content, j'en ai fait venir!

— Ce n'est vraiment pas bon, hein?

* * *

Bianca : Est-ce qu'il faut dire un mensonge ou une menterie?

Jacinthe : Euh...

Bianca : Ni l'un ni l'autre, il faut toujours dire la vérité!

* * *

— François, regarde! Ton chien est en train de lire le journal!

— Non, non. Il fait juste semblant. En réalité, il ne sait pas lire, il regarde juste les photos.

* * *

— Maman! Regarde comme je suis gentil! Je partage avec mon petit frère. Je mange des arachides et je lui donne toutes les écales!

* * *

La prof : Aujourd'hui, nous allons parler des fractions. Si je coupe une feuille de papier en deux, qu'est-ce que j'obtiens?

Les élèves : Des moitiés de feuille!

La prof : Très bien. Et si je la coupe en quatre?

Les élèves : Des quarts!

La prof : C'est ça. Et si je la coupe en huit?

Les élèves : Des huitièmes!

La prof : C'est très très bien! On continue. Si je coupe la feuille en mille, qu'est-ce que j'obtiens?

Les élèves : Des confettis!

* * *

Dans le métro, un homme lit son journal. Chaque fois qu'il finit une page, il la déchire, en fait une petite boulette et la jette par terre.

— Pourquoi faites-vous ça? lui demande Maude.

— C'est pour éloigner les crocodiles.

— Mais il n'y a pas de crocodile ici!

— C'est efficace, hein?

* * *

Après la première journée d'école de Samuel :

— Est-ce que tu as aimé ta journée? lui demande sa mère.

— Oui, mais il y a une chose bizarre.

— Quoi?

— Tu m'avais dit qu'à l'école il ne fallait pas parler. Pourtant, il y a dans ma classe une madame qui n'a pas arrêté de parler de toute la journée!

* * *

Perdu dans le désert par une nuit noire, un petit hérisson frappe un cactus par accident. Il s'exclame, le cœur chaviré :

— Pardon, mademoiselle! Comme vous avez la peau douce!

* * *

Francis : Sais-tu que je suis capable de faire une chose que personne d'autre dans l'école ne peut faire? Même pas les professeurs.

Élaine : Ah oui! Quoi donc?

Francis : Lire mon écriture.

* * *

— Crois-tu que les gens aiment la grande musique?

— Oui, j'en suis certaine!

— Qu'est-ce qui te fait dire ça?

— Je suis allée voir un concert de l'orchestre symphonique en fin de semaine. Eh bien, il y avait tellement de monde que le chef d'orchestre a dû passer toute la soirée debout!

* * *

— Hé! toi! Aimes-tu la crème glacée?

— Non!

— Parfait! Veux-tu tenir mon cornet pendant que j'attache mon soulier?

* * *

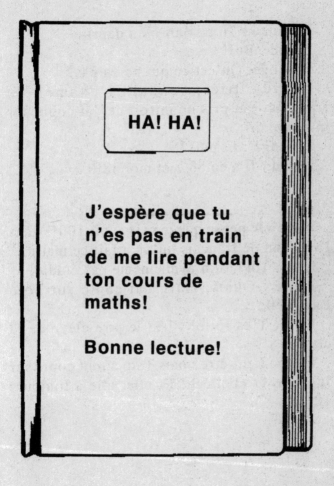

Rosange : Tu as l'air bien déprimé.

David : Bof!

Rosange: Qu'est-ce qui ne va pas?

David : Hier, pendant l'examen de français, j'ai pris un miroir et j'ai copié sur mon voisin.

Rosange : Et puis?

David : Il a eu 83% et moi 38%...

* * *

Flore : Je pense que je vais avoir 100% dans l'examen de français qu'on a fait ce matin.

Lisa : Toi? Tu n'avais même pas étudié!

Flore : Ouais, mais j'ai copié sur Toto Labretelle.

Lisa : T'es folle! C'est le pire élève de la classe!

Flore : Peut-être, mais Toto a tout copié sur Jasmine la «bollée»! Et elle, elle a toujours 100%!

* * *

— Il y a vraiment un drôle de bruit dans mon moteur.

— Et vous y avez vu?

— Oui, je suis d'abord allé au garage de l'autre côté de la rue.

— Ah oui? Et quel mauvais conseil cet imbécile vous a-t-il donné?

— Il m'a dit de venir vous voir!

* * *

— Mon médecin m'a dit de changer toute mon alimentation. Plus de biscuits, de fromage, de crème glacée, de gâteaux, et plus de croustilles.

— Pauvre toi, qu'est-ce que tu vas faire?

— Je vais changer de médecin!

* * *

Pourquoi vaut-il mieux ne pas se promener dans la jungle entre cinq heures et cinq heures et demie?

Parce que c'est l'heure où les éléphants descendent des arbres.

* * *

Pourquoi les alligators ont-ils la tête plate?

C'est parce qu'ils se promènent dans la jungle entre cinq heures et cinq heures et demie!

* * *

Sébastien revient de l'école le pantalon tout déchiré et la jambe passablement amochée.

— Mais que t'est-il arrivé, mon chéri? s'exclame sa mère.

— C'est le chien à côté de l'école qui m'a mordu.

— Mais as-tu mis quelque chose sur ta jambe?

— Non, le chien l'a trouvée très bonne comme ça.

* * *

Deux amis discutent dans la cour de récréation :

— À quelle heure te réveilles-tu, toi, le matin?

— Oh, environ une heure après le début des cours!

* * *

Monsieur Vézina est à l'épicerie. Il a oublié ses lunettes et n'arrive pas à lire la dernière chose que sa femme a inscrite sur la liste. Il demande au boucher de lui dire ce qui est écrit au bas de la note.

Le boucher, un peu gêné, lui chuchote :

— Je t'aime, mon gros poussin adoré!

* * *

À la clinique :

— Docteur, c'est terrible!

— Qu'est-ce qu'il y a?

— Il y a des concombres qui me poussent dans l'oreille!

— En effet, c'est plutôt surprenant!

— Je comprends! Moi qui avais planté des haricots!

* * *

Je suis un nez qui vit collé sur les oreilles. Un nez-couteur!

* * *

L'accordeur de pianos sonne chez madame Grimard.

— Mais je ne vous ai pas fait demander! s'étonne-t-elle.

— Vous, non, mais vos voisins, oui!

* * *

Trois gars font un concours. Celui qui réussit à rester le plus longtemps dans la porcherie gagne.

Le premier entre et ressort en courant au bout de 30 secondes.

Le deuxième prend son souffle et entre. Il ne réussit même pas à rester 15 secondes!

Le troisième entre à son tour. Quinze secondes passent, puis 20, puis 30, et tous les cochons sortent en courant!

* * *

Juliette : Salut! Il paraît que ton voisin s'est acheté un chien de garde?

Xavier : Oui.

Juliette : Est-ce qu'il est efficace?

Xavier : Je comprends qu'il est efficace! Ça fait trois jours que mon voisin essaie de rentrer chez lui!

* * *

Émilie : Pourquoi ta mère porte-t-elle toujours ton petit frère dans ses bras?

Jacinthe : Parce que mon petit frère ne peut pas se porter tout seul!

* * *

Deux amies discutent :
— Ma mère est vraiment bizarre.
— Comment ça?
— Tous les soirs, alors que je ne suis pas fatiguée, elle me couche. Et chaque matin, alors que je suis en train de dormir, elle me réveille!

* * *

Un bon jeudi matin à l'école :
— Tout le monde est en forme? demande le professeur. Ce matin, nous allons étudier les fractions. Si je coupe une pêche en quatre, que j'en mange deux morceaux et que je t'en donne deux, que reste-t-il?
— Il reste le noyau!

* * *

— Qu'est-ce qui est jaune et qui va très vite?
— Je ne sais pas.
— Une banane de course.

* * *

— Sais-tu pourquoi les chats font «miaou»?
— Non.
— C'est parce que s'ils faisaient «wouf», ils seraient des chiens!

* * *

Un homme se présente chez un directeur de cirque.

— Bonjour!

— Qu'est-ce que je peux faire pour vous? demande le directeur.

— Bien voilà : je suis imitateur d'oiseaux. Voulez-vous une démonstration?

— Non, non, ça va. Ce n'est pas nouveau, imiter les oiseaux. J'ai déjà vu des centaines et des centaines de numéros comme ça.

— Peut-être, mais sûrement pas comme le mien! Tant pis! soupire l'homme en s'envolant par la fenêtre.

* * *

— Qu'est-ce qui est transparent et qui sent la banane?

— Je ne sais pas.

— Un pet de singe.

* * *

Un loup et un mouton entrent au restaurant et s'installent à une table.

— Bonjour, dit le serveur. Qu'est-ce que je peux vous servir?

— Je vais prendre un bol de foin et une petite assiette de trèfle, répond le mouton.

— Très bien. Et pour votre ami?

— Il ne prend rien.

— Il n'a pas faim? demande le serveur, surpris.

— Pensez-vous vraiment que je serais avec lui s'il avait faim?

* * *

Coralie : J'aimerais tellement avoir un chat!

Kim : Est-ce que tes parents accepteraient?

Coralie : Non, c'est ça le problème! Ils ne veulent absolument pas laisser un chat entrer dans la maison.

Kim : Et ton frère, lui?

Coralie : Oh, lui, ils le laissent entrer.

* * *

— Sais-tu pourquoi les girafes se mettent du vernis rouge sur les ongles d'orteil?

— Non.

— C'est pour pouvoir se cacher dans les champs de fraises.

— Franchement! Qu'est-ce que tu racontes?

— As-tu déjà vu une girafe dans un champ de fraises?

— Non.

— Non, tu vois, ça marche.

***

Jessica : Aujourd'hui c'est mon anniversaire! Je suis tellement heureuse! Je me sens transformée! J'aurais envie de faire des folies! De faire des choses que je n'ai jamais faites avant!

La mère : Que dirais-tu de faire le ménage de ta chambre?

* * *

Fanny : Connais-tu la différence entre l'école et une pile?

Joël : Non.

Fanny : La pile, elle, a un côté positif!

* * *

Toc! toc! toc!
— Qui est là?
— L.
— L qui?
— L avait très hâte aux vacances!

* * *

La mère : C'est donc bien long! Je t'ai juste demandé de remplir la salière!

Le fils : Mais maman, c'est difficile de faire rentrer les grains par ces petits trous!

* * *

Micheline : Sais-tu quelle est la distance entre la Lune et la Terre?

Le père : Euh... non, je ne le sais pas.

Micheline : Alors, ne viens pas me gronder si j'ai une mauvaise note pour mon devoir. Ce sera ta faute!

* * *

Claudiane : Est-ce que je peux aller aux toilettes?

Le prof : Bien sûr. Et si tu vois le directeur, dis-lui que je veux lui parler.

Claudiane : D'accord. Et si je ne le vois pas, qu'est-ce que je lui dis?

* * *

Yves : C'est vrai que tu es sorti de la classe en plein milieu de l'après-midi?

Bernard : Oui, après ce que la prof m'avait dit, il n'était pas question que je reste une seconde de plus!

Yves : Mais que t'a-t-elle dit?

Bernard : «Au bureau du directeur tout de suite!»

* * *

Claudia : Quand je mange trop de chocolat, je n'arrive pas à m'endormir.

Marco : C'est drôle, moi c'est le contraire. Quand je dors, je n'arrive pas à manger du chocolat!

* * *

Danika : Sais-tu que les perruques et toi vous avez beaucoup de choses en commun?

Nathalie : Ah oui! Comment ça?

Danika : Eh bien tous les deux vous avez beaucoup de cheveux et pas de tête!

* * *

— Que faisaient les invités de Mozart pour lui faire savoir qu'ils étaient arrivés?

— Je ne sais pas.

— Ils appuyaient sur la sonate!

* * *

La gardienne : Mais voyons, Jérémie! Pourquoi as-tu mordu ta sœur?

Jérémie : Un instant! Je ne l'ai pas mordue!

La gardienne : Ah non? Qu'est-ce que tu viens juste de faire, alors?

Jérémie : Je l'ai embrassée avec les dents!

* * *

— Qui est la personne qui connaît le plus de secrets à l'école?

— Je ne sais pas.

— La SECRETaire!

* * *

Myriam : C'est l'histoire d'une tortue qui s'en va à La Ronde.

Anne-Sophie : Oui, et que lui arrive-t-il?

Myriam : Un instant, laisse-lui le temps de se rendre!

* * *

Deux copains discutent :

— Est-ce que ta mère porte des lunettes?

— Elle devrait en porter, mais elle ne les met jamais.

— Pourquoi?

— Pour ne pas voir toutes les niaiseries que je fais dans une journée!

* * *

Toc! toc! toc!
— Qui est là?
— C.
— C qui?
— C juste une blague!

* * *

Blaise :
Sais-tu
ce qu'on
recueille
quand on
trait une
vache
stressée?
Pascale :
Non.
Blaise :
Du lait
fouetté!

* * *

Le directeur reçoit dans son bureau deux élèves qui se sont battus dans la cour de récréation.

— Victor, est-ce que c'est vrai que tu as cassé une raquette de badminton sur la tête de Gilberto?

— Oui, mais je ne l'ai pas fait exprès!

— Ah, il me semblait bien! Tu ne voulais pas faire mal à Gilberto!

— Non, Monsieur, je ne voulais pas briser la raquette!

* * *

Charles : Mon chat a remporté le premier prix d'un concours de beauté pour oiseaux.

Hubert : Pour oiseaux! Comment ça?

Charles : Il a bouffé le perroquet qui avait gagné le premier prix!

* * *

À l'école, le directeur cherche un élève qui pourra le seconder dans un projet d'aide aux plus jeunes. Agatha se rend au bureau du directeur pour poser sa candidature.

Le directeur : Comme ça, tu crois que tu peux m'aider dans cette tâche?

Agatha : Oh oui!

Le directeur : Tu sais, j'ai besoin de quelqu'un de très responsable!

Agatha : Alors je suis sûre de faire l'affaire!

Le directeur : Comment ça?

Agatha : Dans ma classe, mon prof m'a dit que chaque fois qu'il y a quelque chose qui cloche, c'est moi la responsable!

* * *

La petite tortue dit à sa mère :

— Je m'en vais jouer chez mon ami; je reviendrai dans trois semaines!

* * *

— Connais-tu la blague de l'imbécile qui disait toujours non?

— Non!

* * *

Monsieur Faucher arrive au ciel. On lui demande ce qui lui est arrivé.

— J'étais en voyage en train de traverser une rivière infestée d'alligators. Soudain, un câble du petit pont suspendu a lâché et le pont a basculé! Mais heureusement tout le monde a réussi à s'accrocher à la rampe. Malheureusement, nous étions trop nombreux et la rampe menaçait de se briser. Le guide nous a dit : «Quelqu'un va devoir se sacrifier et sauter pour sauver les autres.» Finalement, un homme s'est laissé tomber.

— Mais pourquoi êtes-vous ici au ciel si tout s'est bien terminé?

— Le guide nous a dit que cet homme courageux méritait bien qu'on l'applaudisse...

* * *

CONCOURS

Tu dois connaître, toi aussi, de courtes histoires drôles. Alors, pourquoi ne pas nous en faire parvenir quelques-unes?

Parmi celles reçues, certaines seront retenues pour publication et l'auteur(e) recevra une surprise.

Participe le plus vite possible et envoie tes histoires drôles à :

CONCOURS HISTOIRES DRÔLES
Les éditions Héritage inc.
300, rue Arran
Saint-Lambert (Québec)
J4R 1K5

Nous avons hâte de te lire!
                              À très bientôt donc!

Payette & Simms inc.

Achevé d'imprimer en septembre 2001 sur les presses de
Payette & Simms inc. à Saint-Lambert (Québec)

CATARRH

Advice on diet, exercise and natural
treatments for the relief of catarrhal
symptoms.

By the same author

THE NEW SELF HELP SERIES

CATARRH

TRIED AND TESTED
NATUROPATHIC METHODS FOR
TREATING CATARRHAL CONDITIONS

ARTHUR WHITE
ND DO

Thorsons
An Imprint of HarperCollinsPublishers

Thorsons
An Imprint of HarperCollins*Publishers*
77–85 Fulham Palace Road,
Hammersmith, London W6 8JB.

Published by Thorsons 1987
7 9 10 8 6

Arthur White asserts the moral right to
be identified as the author of this work

British Library Cataloguing in Publication Data

White, Arthur, 1914–
Thorsons new self help for catarrh
1. Catarrh
I. Title
616.2   RC741

ISBN 0-7225-1381-X

Printed in Great Britain by
HarperCollins Manufacturing, Glasgow

Contents

Note to reader

1.

Catarrh – the Ubiquitous Malady

The word 'catarrh' is derived from a Greek term meaning 'to flow down' – an apt description of the persistent secretion of mucus which characterizes what, in the United Kingdom and many other industrial communities, is undoubtedly one of the most common afflictions among young and old alike.

There are probably very few people who, at one time or another during the year, do not need to have recourse to the frequent nose-blowing, coughing and throat-clearing necessitated by an excessive 'flowing down' of mucus.

Indeed, so universal is this particular problem that it is widely regarded as a normal, though sometimes inconvenient, bodily function, and has given birth to a multi-million pound industry devoted to the production of what are euphemistically known as toilet tissues.

The relatively mild symptoms are, however, but the tip of an enormous iceberg of other and very much more serious catarrhal problems which tend to develop slowly and insidiously over the years and which can affect tissues and organs throughout the body.

The seeds of these disorders are often sown in infancy and early schooldays when such acute childish illnesses as 'snuffles', colds, measles, whooping-cough and tonsillitis are looked upon as an inevitable concomitant of the growing-up process.

During adolescence, hay-fever is a common affliction, and many young people suffer the acute embarassment and psychological stress which result from skin and scalp disorders such as acne, boils, dandruff and greasy hair. Although these are not regarded as 'catarrhal complaints in the accepted sense of the term, they derive from the same basic causes.

It is, however, among adults, and particularly the older age-groups, that the more serious manifestations of chronic catarrh begin to appear, largely because little or no effort has been made by the orthodox health authorities to identify the true nature of the problem. As a result, the colds and coughs which characterize the early phases of catarrhal congestion are regarded as simple virus infections and do not warrant a visit to the doctor's consulting-room which, in any case, would result only in an injunction to take things easy, keep warm and perhaps take a couple of aspirins every four hours or so.

In the terms of a frequently quoted witticism, the average cold will clear in two weeks with medical treatment, or 14 days without it. This is in effect a tacit recognition of the fact that the body's own self-healing powers are quite capable of dealing effectively with any such acute illnesses without – or even in spite of – outside help or interference.

Unfortunately, both the patient and his or her medical advisers look no further than the mysterious 'virus' being responsible for the symptoms, and so, as we shall explain later, no attempt is made to eradicate the real cause of the colds and coughs. As a result of this short-sighted attitude, once some semblance of health has been restored, the patient resumes what is regarded as a normal way of life, blissfully unaware that in so doing he will be setting the scene for another and possibly more serious 'infection' in the future.

When, as is almost inevitable, this sequence of events has been allowed to recur at varying intervals over a period of many years, the body's ability to deal speedily and effectively with the problem is progressively weakened, so that the congestion and inflammation spread from the nose and throat to the mucous membranes which line other vital organs.

The lungs are probably and understandably one of the most vulnerable organs in this respect because of their close association with the nose and throat, and it is not surprising that bronchitis is a major cause of death, particularly among the elderly. Indeed, this disease alone is responsible for so many fatalities in this country that it has been termed 'the English disease'.

The middle ear and the sinuses are perhaps even more vulnerable than the lungs to the malevolent repercussions to which chronic catarrh may give rise. The former is connected to the back of the throat via a narrow canal – the Eustachian tube – the function of which is to allow air to enter the middle-ear cavity so that atmospheric pressure remains constant on both sides of the ear-drum. It is approximately 3cms (1½ ins) in length and is lined with mucous membrane which is a continuation of that which protects the nose and throat. Therefore, if any catarrhal involvement of the latter is not dealt with effectively, the resultant inflammation of the mucous membranes will gradually extend into the Eustachian tube causing increasing congestion which will progressively narrow and eventually block the connective canal. Once this occurs, the tiny chamber of the middle ear will be effectively sealed, and because the vibratory capacity of the ear-drum will be reduced, some degree of deafness will result.

As a further complication of this state of affairs, increasing congestion in the middle ear may give rise to abscess formation and rupture of the ear-drum, while disruption of the delicate mechanisms of the middle ear may give rise to distressing head-noises – tinnitus – which, it has been claimed, afflict no less than eight million people in the UK alone.

Sinusitis is another very common affliction which stems from chronic catarrh and which may give rise to a variety of painful symptoms including headache, a sensation of pressure in the temples, and pain in the cheekbones and behind the eyes.

The sinuses are four pairs of cavities in the skull in the vicinity of the nose which, in addition to reducing the weight of the bony structure, are believed to help in warming and moistening the air during inspiration. For the latter purpose they all connect with the nasal air passages and are lined with mucous membrane, and so, like the Eustachian tube, they are very susceptible to catarrhal involvement.

Another all-too-common manifestation of catarrh, particularly in children, is tonsillitis, which means inflammation of the two small glands situated at the entrance to the throat. As is the case with the many other glands in various parts of the system, the tonsils play a very important role in protecting the body from harmful organisms and purifying the blood-stream. Consequently, any infection of the adjacent tissues will increase the work-load on the tonsils and they will become enlarged in an effort to cope with the extra burden. During the first half of the twentieth century it was the almost invariable practice of the orthodox medical profession to surgically remove enlarged tonsils, and it was only after many thousands of children had been mutilated in this way that the futility of this short-sighted operation was recognized and the practice was largely abandoned.

The malign effects of chronic catarrh are by no means confined to the tissues and organs in the vicinity of the nose and throat, but can involve any hollow organ which has a mucous lining, including the gall-bladder (cholecystitis), the stomach (gastritis), the bowels (diverticulitis, appendicitis, colitis, proctitis), and the urinary organs (cystitis, urethritis).

It may have surprised many readers to learn that what is usually regarded as being a common and relatively mild complaint can, in the long term, have such widespread and potentially serious repercussions, and the regrettable fact is that this sorry state of affairs would not exist if the true causes of catarrh were recognized and treated rationally by the medical profession instead of their resorting to the use of drugs in an attempt merely to suppress the colds, coughs, influenza, etc. which mark the early phases of the catarrhal problem.

2.

What are Mucous Membranes?

If we are to understand the true nature of catarrh we must first know something about the tissues which are primarily involved, i.e. the mucous membranes – what their functions are, and what causes them to run amok from time to time and inflict upon us the irksome symptoms which characterize catarrh and the frequent colds which are almost invariably its precursor.

As we have already explained, many of the hollow organs of the body – e.g. the air passages, the stomach, the bowels and the bladder – are lined with mucous membrane, and although there may be minor structural differences between them, depending upon the specialized functions which they are required to perform, they all have the common characteristic of being lubricated by mucus. This is a slimy, tenacious material composed largely of a protein called mucin, but also containing a variety of other substances.

The membrane itself consists of fibrous connective tissues similar to the true skin, although it is considerably softer and lighter in texture. In it are situated blood-vessels and nerves, and tiny specialized cells in which the mucus is formed. As these cells fill, they become increasingly distended and eventually burst, discharging their contents onto the surface of the membrane (see Figure 1 opposite).

The tissues with which we are primarily concerned – i.e. the membranes lining the air passages – differ from most of those which cover other internal organs in that their surface is covered with a mass of very fine 'hairs', called cilia, which, by means of a rapid waving movement, propel the mucus along the air passages and out of the body, carrying with it cellular debris, germs, dust and other potentially harmful substances which may have been borne on the inhaled air.

It will be seen, therefore, that in a healthy individual the mucous membranes constitute an ingenious and valuable protective mechanism which, as should be the case with all bodily organs, perform their vital tasks unobtrusively, day in and day out, throughout life.

Under modern living conditions, however, such a state of perfection could well be regarded as impossible of achievement, for reasons which we shall explain later, and there are probably few of us who remain blissfully unaware of the

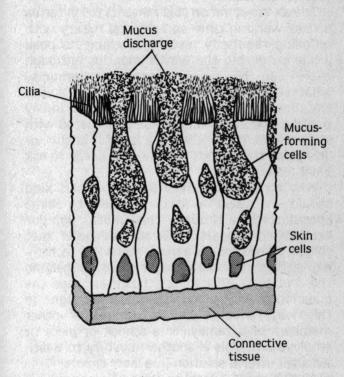

Figure 1. Section through mucous membrane showing cilia and mucus-forming cells.

activities of our mucous membranes from one year to the next.

The all-too-common cold takes its toll in terms of lost working time and physical misery with unfailing regularity, usually reaching its peak incidence during the winter months, although there can be no guarantee of immunity whatever the season. In any community, and at any time of the year, casual conversation in any public gathering is likely to be punctuated with such comments as 'There's a lot of it about', or 'It's going the rounds', and no one needs to ask what 'it' is.

Why a relatively trivial ailment of this kind should be called a 'cold' is open to some speculation, although the most popular explanation appears to favour the belief that chilling of the body is a major causative factor – e.g. sitting in a cold draught of air, or getting the feet wet. This theory, however, begs the question of why a cold, having been 'caught' in this way, should 'go the rounds' of other members of a family, or a school, or place of employment. This is another mystery to which we shall offer a solution in a later chapter.

At this stage, what we wish to emphasize is that over-activity of the mucous membranes, like enlargement of the tonsils, sneezing and coughing, represents an attempt by the living organism to cope with an abnormal situation which poses a threat to its well-being.

Just as a sneeze is triggered in order to expel

a potentially harmful substance from the nose, and a cough is induced to clear mucus or some other obstruction from the throat or lungs, and the tonsils enlarge in order to clear toxic material from the bloodstream, so the activities of the mucous membranes are intensified when the need arises to augment the tissue-cleansing functions of the body's main eliminative organs – i.e. the kidneys, skin, bowels and lungs.

Once it is clearly understood that what are commonly regarded as symptoms of ill health are in fact vital protective mechanisms, it can be readily appreciated that any attempt to 'cure' catarrh, or prevent sneezing or coughing, or reduce enlarged tonsils by means of medicines, inhalants or even surgery, must in the long term prove counter-productive, and sow the seeds of more serious health problems in later life. All of these functions are safety valves which come into operation only in order to cope with emergency situations; therefore, any misguided attempt to close down the safety valves or render them inoperative can only lead to disaster.

3.

Medical
Misconceptions

Throughout the twentieth century medical practice has become increasingly drug orientated, with the result that, today, it is almost universally accepted that any patient who visits a GP's consulting room will come away clutching a prescription for a pill or potion to be dispensed by the local pharmacist.

So universal is this practice that the National Health Service has become burdened with a multi-million pound drug bill which increases remorselessly year after year, despite repeated efforts by successive Health Ministers to achieve some measure of control and economy.

In addition to this vast bill for medically prescribed remedies there is massive public expenditure on non-prescription medicines which are sold over the counter not only in chemists' shops but nowadays in supermarkets and many general stores.

The practice of drug medication is based on

the theory that many common ailments are the result of an attack by germs or viruses and that health can only be restored if the invading organism is destroyed. To this end, a medical pharmacopoeia has been compiled which lists many thousands of drugs and which explains at length the specific uses to which they may be put in order to combat the germs and viruses which, it is fervently believed, are the cause of many of the most common illnesses.

One such volume runs to well over two thousand pages of very small type, including an index of no less than 170 pages.

It is hardly surprising, therefore, that the pharmaceutical industry consists of some of the largest and most wealthy multi-national companies whose turn-over and profits are measured in thousands of millions of pounds.

Amazingly, however, despite enormous public and private expenditure on drugs, the burden of ill health continues to increase. It is true that the incidence of some diseases such as diphtheria, tuberculosis and smallpox has declined over the years, but there is a very good reason to believe that these changes are due not to 'medical progress' but to better hygiene and improved living standards generally.

Against these apparent health benefits must be set the increasing incidence of such diseases as cancer, arthritis, kidney failure, coronary disease and a wide variety of psychological disorders. Not only have orthodox medical efforts failed to produce a cure for these very serious ailments, but there is ample evidence to suggest that the increasingly potent drugs which are prescribed so freely are at least partially responsible for some of these serious degenerative diseases. A substantial part of the medical pharmacopoeia is devoted to the toxic side-effects which may arise during treatment, and doctors are specifically requested to be constantly on the alert for any such untoward symptoms and notify them to a special drug-monitoring committee. It is as a result of this very necessary precaution that, from time to time, a new and presumably extensively tested drug has been 'withdrawn' by the manufacturers following the disclosure of serious and sometimes fatal side-effects.

Perhaps the most telling indictment of the fallacy of orthodox medicine comes from the abject failure of research scientists to find an effective cure for what are undoubtedly some of the simplest and most widespread ailments – namely catarrhal disorders such as colds, influenza, laryngitis, tonsillitis, etc.

As long ago as 1946 the Medical Research Council established the Common Cold Research Unit in Salisbury where, for ten-day periods, volunteer members of the public are isolated from the outside world while being exposed to various conditions which the research workers hope will result in their developing a cold. During their stay they are subjected to a number of investigative procedures, and any who are sufficiently obliging as to 'catch' a germ or virus are required to co-operate further by testing out the curative effects of new drugs.

They are housed in small units, with no personal contacts other than the two or three other inmates sharing their accommodation, and, of course, the research workers who oversee their particular part of the proceedings.

Yet despite all the efforts of the successive teams of trained scientists over so many decades virtually no progress has been made towards identifying the cause of the common cold or finding a drug or vaccine which can be relied upon to cure the victims or protect the man in the street from infection.

The problem, it seems, is that there are so many different viruses which can 'cause' a cold – 150 groups at the last count – all having different characteristics and varying degrees of susceptibility to the complex chemical substances devised by the scientists, that no single nostrum can destroy more than a very small proportion of the infecting organisms, and a vaccine which is thought to be effective against some of the groups is totally impotent in respect of most of the others.

Efforts have also been made to test the validity of some of the traditional theories concerning the causes of colds with equally disappointing results. It was found that, contrary to popular belief, volunteers who were exposed to cold draughts or wintry weather conditions, or whose feet had been allowed to remain cold and wet for varying periods, were no more likely to succumb to infection than others who led a more coddled existence.

One faint glimmer of light that emerged as a result of the Salisbury experiments showed that a virus will only succeed in infecting an individual in whom it finds the right conditions in which it can thrive and multiply. Such conditions, it was concluded, are likely to be found in those who are somewhat run down in general health or who have been subjected to some form of physical or emotional stress.

It seems, therefore, to be a sad reflection on the health of the public as a whole that it is estimated that children may suffer as many as six or seven colds every year, and that in adults the infection-rate is in the region of twice yearly.

Apparently, the degree of susceptibility to the common cold is in inverse ratio to a person's age, with the frequency of infection falling progressively from infancy to old age. The 'scientific' explanation for this phenomenon is that once the body has been infected it develops antibodies which are able to protect it from whichever of the various virus types was responsible for the attack. Although the resultant immunity tends to diminish with the passage of time, it is argued that at any one time some 50% of the adult population will enjoy some degree of protection against the depredations of any one of the many different types of virus. Following this line of reasoning, it is argued that young people, on the other hand, will not have developed the same degree of antibody protection, and that their suscepti-bility to infection will be further increased because of their greater proclivity to herd together in schools, clubs, etc.

In a later chapter we shall put forward alternative explanations for both the origin of natural immunity and the lessening frequency of infection by the common-cold virus which comes with the ageing process.

Meanwhile, the purveyors of medicines for the relief of the many catarrhal afflictions continue to reap a rich harvest of profit from a market estimated to be worth in excess of one hundred million pounds annually – a figure which represents only the amount spent by the public in chemists and other retail outlets, and does not include the cost of drugs supplied against doctors' prescriptions through the National Health Service.

At any one time it is likely that the shelves of a moderately well-stocked chemist's shop will contain no fewer than fifty colourfully packaged products ranging from simple cough lozenges to very sophisticated combinations of drugs aimed at relieving practically all the common cold symptoms at one fell swoop.

It is significant, however, that in all the

ingenious advertising for these products which features daily in the popular press and on commercial television throughout the peak months of the common-cold season, there is never a direct claim that any one of these remedies will actually *cure* a cold. Nor is there any indication that any benefit derived from their use will almost certainly be short-lived and that any such temporary local relief may be more than outweighed by detrimental effects on other bodily organs and systems.

For example, among the most widely advertised products are those which are claimed to relieve congestion and clear a blocked-up nose, either in the form of a syrup or a tablet to be taken internally, or sprays or drops which give off a vapour.

The former enter the bloodstream via the stomach and shrink the swollen blood-vessels which are causing nasal congestion, but if they are used continuously for more than a few days a reaction may arise as a result of which the symptoms become worse than they were before treatment commenced.

Some of these medicines contain an antihistamine – a chemical which is known to cause headaches and drowsiness in some cases, resulting in a reduced capacity for concentration and clear thinking.

The vapour-rubs and inhalants, on the other hand, act directly on the swollen mucous membranes of the nose and so are less likely to cause any systemic reactions. Their effect is, however, likely to be relatively short-lived, and the same degree of relief would probably be obtained by sniffing a little weak saline solution or the steam from a bowl of hot water.

Proprietary cough syrups are another of the best-sellers among over-the-counter remedies, and here again they are formulated from drugs which enter the bloodstream and stimulate the glands to increase the secretion of mucus so that it may be more easily coughed up. In order to achieve this effect, however, the drugs must have irritant properties and as these cannot be confined specifically to inflamed tissues they can also cause inflammation and congestion of the stomach and other parts of the digestive tract. For this reason they are especially liable to exacerbate gastric ulcers and some other digestive disorders.

A variation on this theme comes in the form of throat pastilles and lozenges many of which are fruit- or mint-flavoured and are made from various combinations of supposedly soothing substances such as glycerine and honey. Some also have anaesthetic and antiseptic properties and may afford some degree of temporary relief from the soreness and irritation. Most, however, contain a sweetening agent, usually sugar, and so, as will be explained later, their long-term effect is inevitably counter-productive.

Sufferers from the more acute feverish

manifestations of the catarrh syndrome are almost invariably advised to go to bed, keep warm and take aspirin from time to time, but even this time-honoured panacea is now known to cause a number of undesirable side-effects including dizziness, head noises, sweating, nausea and vomiting. Even small doses, it has been found, can irritate the stomach lining and so cause digestive disturbances, bleeding and ulceration.

In some sensitive individuals, such as asthma sufferers, aspirin can produce quite dramatic reactions in the form of skin eruptions and breathlessness, and – especially relevant in the context of the subject of this book – bronchial spasm and rhinitis, both of which are manifestations of catarrhal congestion.

We could write at considerably greater length about the futility of trying to cure disease and restore health by means of such totally illogical procedures as the administration of potentially poisonous drugs, but we feel that sufficient has been said to persuade the reader that there must be a safer and more rational approach to the all-too-common problems of catarrhal ailments.

The fundamental principle upon which this alternative approach is based requires that we shall first identify the *true* causes of ill health and then take steps to correct or remove them. In the next chapter, therefore, we shall dispose of the myth that germs and viruses are the primary cause of infectious diseases, as a preliminary to offering a more logical alternative explanation of the events and practices which pave the way for the onset of the all-too-familiar symptoms of catarrhal ailments.

4.

The Misunderstood Microbe

From earliest childhood most of us were indoctrinated into believing that the many infectious illnesses such as measles, chicken-pox, scarlet fever, poliomyelitis, influenza and various other feverish ailments are the inevitable result of an 'attack' on the body by an invading organism.

Louis Pasteur was mainly responsible for establishing the concept that specific germs were the primary cause of specific diseases, and since he propounded his theories, in the middle years of the nineteenth century, orthodox medical practice has been largely dominated by the belief that many diseases can only be cured or prevented by administering a drug or vaccine which will kill whatever variety of bacterium is found to be present in the afflicted patient.

Over the years what was originally termed the 'germ theory' of disease causation has had to be modified in the light of the realization that germs could be present in the human body without there being any of the symptoms of the disease which they were supposed to cause. Moreover, just when it was thought that a drug had been discovered which could kill off the germ of a particular disease another microscopic organism appeared on the scene which 'caused' virtually the same symptoms but which was totally unharmed by the new drug.

Even more disconcerting was the realization that the bacteria which are associated with disease symptoms are comparatively few in number, and that the vast majority of the micro-organisms found in nature are either completely harmless to humans, or beneficial, or even essential to bodily health. Not surprisingly, it soon became apparent that any drug that is potent enough to kill off a harmful germ would inevitably prove equally lethal to other organisms, quite apart from the harmful side-effects to which all drugs give rise and to which we referred in the previous chapter.

Unfortunately, these revelations did little to persuade medical researchers to revise their views concerning the cause of infectious diseases, and they merely redoubled their efforts to discover a magic formula which would enable them to dispose of the delinquent bacteria while causing the least possible damage to the patient.

As it became patently obvious that the germ could no longer be indicted as the primary cause of infectious illness another scapegoat had to be produced, and with the development of more highly sophisticated microscopes the researchers discovered the viruses – minute living structures that are so small that they could pass undetected through the porcelain filters which had been used to isolate other micro-organisms. It is difficult for any layman to contemplate the existence of a living entity of such incredibly small dimensions that many thousands of bacteria could be located on the tiniest visible speck of dust. Yet each bacterium may be up to *three hundred times larger* than a virus which only becomes visible with the aid of a powerful electron microscope.

With the discovery of viruses the germs have been relegated to a lower division of medical research, although they are still regarded as being primarily responsible for a variety of diseases, including diphtheria, dysentery, tuberculosis, whooping-cough, boils and carbuncles, and various feverish illnesses.

So far as the majority of infectious illnesses are concerned, however, it is the normally invisible virus which is now regarded as the principal enemy, and medical research is orientated largely towards finding a drug which can destroy these malign organisms without causing too much injury to the patient.

It is a quest that is doomed to inevitable failure for several reasons. In the first place, as we have already stressed, any drug which is sufficiently toxic to destroy one form of living entity will inevitably prove fatal to others which need to be nurtured. Even the most dedicated research chemist will be compelled to admit that, because of this very inconvenient characteristic, there can be no such substance as a totally safe drug, and that the best that they can hope for is that they may discover a medicine the beneficial effects of which are likely to outweigh its toxic side-effects.

As if this alone were not a sufficiently daunting test of their ingenuity, they are faced with a further problem that viruses differ fundamentally in many ways. Consequently, a medicine that is toxic to a certain type of virus will have no appreciable effect on the others which make up the vast variety of supposedly harmful organisms.

The same problem has bedevilled scientists who have endeavoured to discover a vaccine which would afford immunity to colds and influenza. Not surprisingly, they have failed to evolve a substance which can give effective protection against the 150 groups of viruses which are held to be responsible for the common cold, and their efforts to ward off attacks of influenza have proved equally abortive because each successive epidemic of this acute feverish illness appears to be characterized by the presence in the victims of a different strain of virus.

Moreover, these ingenious organisms have a

tiresome habit of achieving immunity to the antibiotics and other drugs which have been used to combat their forebears.

It is much more than a century since Louis Pasteur first expounded the theory that specific germs are the cause of specific diseases and yet despite all the efforts and ingenuity of our most talented research scientists no one has yet succeeded in devising a drug or vaccine which can prevent or cure infectious diseases by killing off the suspected microbe.

Surely then, it is logical to suspect that such total failure must call into question the whole concept upon which the germ theory of disease causation is founded and to look for an alternative explanation of the relationship which undoubtedly exists between the symptoms of catarrhal ailments such as colds, coughs and influenza and the germs or viruses which are undeservedly held to be responsible for their onset.

As early as the first decades of the twentieth century the pioneers of natural healing – notably Stanley Lief and James C. Thomson – were challenging the validity of the orthodox medical view that acute disease could be 'caught' through infection and that it could be transmitted from one person to another via bacteria or viruses.

They did not question the *existence* of these micro-organisms, but they did insist that a fundamental error had been made in assuming that because a germ or virus was found to be present in the body of a sufferer from an infectious disease it was necessarily the cause of the malady. It was, they insisted, a 'chicken or the egg' situation and they maintained that contrary to the theory that the presence of the germs was *ipso facto* the cause of the disease, the true situation was that pre-existing conditions in the sick patient's body provided the environmental state within the tissues which allowed the bacteria to flourish and multiply.

Only if this explanation is accepted is it possible to explain why only a relatively small percentage of those who come into contact with an infectious person subsequently succumb to the illness, and why the germs of a disease such as tuberculosis or diphtheria can be found to be present in the body of a person who exhibits none of the symptoms of that disease.

The fact is that these micro-organisms exist in such vast numbers in all living tissues that they are literally all-pervading. If, as medical scientists insist on maintaining, even a small proportion of them have the capability of causing disease then the entire creature population would long since have been wiped out.

Why, then, has such a calamity not overtaken us? The answer is simple – so simple, in fact, that the research scientists, totally preoccupied with their electron-microscopes and their quest for the elusive predatory microbe, cannot recognize the logical hypothesis that illness starts and develops *within* the body and that the presence of bacteria in the tissues is the *result* of disease *and not its cause.*

The extent of this scientific blindness is exemplified by the fact that, as we have mentioned in an earlier chapter, research into the causes of the common cold had established that, in order to 'catch' a cold, it is not sufficient merely to be exposed to an infecting organism, but that the body of the potential victim should also provide the germ or virus with the right environmental conditions which they need in order to thrive.

In other words, a bacterium which invades a healthy body will be powerless to initiate any disease process, but if instead it has the good fortune to enter the bloodstream of someone who is generally run down and debilitated it will proliferate rapidly.

On the basis of this realization, the naturopathic pioneers deduced that not only were bacteria an effect of disease and not its cause, but that they were in fact scavengers which played a vital role in cleansing unhealthy tissue of toxic residues and that once this function had been fulfilled they departed, leaving the body cleansed – and 'cured'.

In nature, nothing that happens is without some constructive purpose. Nothing is lost, and nothing is wasted. Naturopaths recognize this fundamental truth and use it as a basis on which to achieve an understanding of the symptoms of disease, their causes, and the ways in which the body's very effective powers of self-healing can be mobilized in order to restore health and rebuild damaged tissues and organs.

Such a concept enables them to recognize that it is the debilitated state of the body which is responsible for the presence of what are popularly regarded as 'disease germs' and not vice versa.

In the natural order of things there is a never-ending cycle by means of which the elements, of which all animate and inanimate organisms are composed, are utilized, broken down and utilized again. We see this process in action over and over again in everyday life.

A seed is planted in the soil, where it sends out roots which take up minerals in solution; these are used to form the stems, leaves, flowers and seeds of a plant which matures and eventually dies. Within a very short time the various components of the dead plant disappear from the surface of the earth, having been consumed by worms, slugs, insects and moulds by which they are digested and broken down into a variety of materials, some of which are used to nourish the consumer while the remainder are excreted and returned to the soil.

Similarly, the consuming organism will eventually die and its body will in turn 'decompose' into the various elements of which its tissues were constructed.

Thus the mineral elements which were taken

from the soil by the seed are all returned to the soil, and the same process will be repeated from season to season, year after year in an unending cycle of construction, decomposition and reconstruction.

It is the same process which the gardener utilizes when he builds a compost heap. The leaves, weeds, grass-cuttings, etc. which are stacked into the bin are 'digested' by a teeming army of visible and invisible living organisms, and in due time the bin in emptied and a supply of mineral-rich black 'humus' is spread around the garden to nourish another generation of plants.

The worms, slugs, insects and moulds in the compost-bin are analogous to the germs which operate within the body and which perform the vital function of 'digesting' cell waste and potentially harmful toxic residues. Therefore, it is clearly illogical and misguided to administer drugs to a sick person in order to kill the bacteria and thus halt a vital tissue-cleansing process which nature has set in motion as part of an essential, constructive cycle of events the object of which is to restore health and chemical equilibrium in an ailing organism.

We know that if food residues are left too long in the larder they will soon begin to decompose and give off a very offensive odour and attract swarms of flies which will lay their eggs on the decaying food. Maggots will hatch from the eggs and consume the rotting material. If, however, we kill off the flies by spraying them with an insecticide and do not remove the stale food it will continue to pollute the air in the larder. Clearly, it is no more logical to argue that because flies are always found on tainted food they caused the food to go bad than it is to assume that because a certain type of germ is found in the tissues of a bronchitic it is the cause of the patient's illness.

The flies and the germs were attracted by the 'rubbish' that needed to be disposed of, and so, instead of fighting and destroying them we should concentrate all our efforts on disposing of the offensive debris as speedily as possible. Once that has been achieved the scavengers will depart, their purpose in the natural order of things having been fulfilled.

If we have appeared to labour this particular point it is because it illustrates so clearly what is undoubtedly one of the fundamental differences between the orthodox medical theory concerning the nature and causes of disease and that of the naturopath.

The former concentrates his efforts almost exclusively on the task of relieving symptoms, primarily by prescribing drugs, all of which are known to be harmful to a greater or lesser degree. When this line of attack fails and the patient's condition continues to deteriorate he then resorts to surgery in order to remove

organs and tissues which, as a result of
continual misuse and abuse, have degenerated
beyond any hope of redemption.

The naturopath, on the other hand, regards
symptoms only as the end-result of deep-seated
and possibly long-sustained disturbances of
systemic equilibrium. His primary concern,
therefore, is to identify the *causes* of the
symptoms and either remove or correct them,
knowing that when this objective has been
achieved the body's innate capacity for repair
and self-healing will be brought fully into play to
restore health.

The medical profession sets out to fight
disease and suppress symptoms, whereas the
naturopath co-operates with the natural forces
within the body which alone can 'cure' disease;
once the causes are removed, the relief of
symptoms will follow as an inevitable
consequence.

If, therefore, we have now cleared away some
of the age-old myths and misconceptions
concerning catarrhal disorders, we can now turn
the coin over, so to speak, and explain why it is
that failure to recognize the true nature of
minor acute ailments in early life opens the door
to the very much more serious manifestations
of chronic catarrh in later years.

5.

The Origins of Catarrh

In its simplest form catarrh reveals its presence through a cold in the head, characterized by a thin discharge, blocked nostrils, watering eyes and frequent sneezing. These symptoms, which usually peak within three or four days and then gradually subside, have one thing in common – namely, that they are primarily of an excretory nature, serving to expel from the air passages an abnormally profuse flow of mucus secreted by the tiny glands in the membranes of the nose and throat. These secretions, in turn, are utilized by the body as a vehicle for the removal from its tissues of cell debris and potentially harmful substances with which it has become overburdened and with which the normal organs of elimination – the bowels, the kidneys, the lungs and the skin – are no longer able to cope.

If this toxic burden is light and the emergency measures are allowed to complete their task unhindered, the cold symptoms will abate quickly and the patient's general health will have benefited as a result of the 'spring-cleaning' procedures. But if, as is all too often the case, suppressive medication and other measures are employed in order to 'cure' the cold, the body's eliminative efforts will be thwarted and any toxic materials which have not already been cleared from the system will be forced back into the tissues.

In most cases the acute symptoms will then simmer on for a few days and gradually subside completely, but eventually the body will reassert its determination to rid itself of the toxic burden and another cold will 'break out'.

As we have observed in a previous chapter, these eliminative crises, as they are known in naturopathic circles, are more common and often more acute in children and young people, and they tend to become less frequent and severe with increasing age. The orthodox medical explanation for this phenomenon is that children and adolescents tend to congregate more freely in large groups and so run a greater risk of infection. Moreover, it is claimed that once the body has been infected by a virus it has the ability to develop antibodies which can protect it for a time from further attacks by the same micro-organism, and this, it is suggested, also helps to explain the greater susceptibility of young people who will have had fewer opportunities to acquire antibody protection.

We have already made the point that if

infection by a germ or virus was in fact primarily responsible for the spread of infectious disease no one would be immune to many serious and often fatal maladies. Nor is it possible to explain why some adults suffer a succession of colds, coughs and other catarrhal illnesses, despite the supposed ability of the body to acquire antibody protection.

Clearly, there must be a more tenable explanation for these apparent anomalies and here, again, the naturopaths have an alternative theory to offer.

Acute illnesses, they are convinced, are in effect an emergency safety-valve as we have already suggested. The speed and efficiency with which these measures are brought into operation are proportional to the degree of health and vitality of the individual concerned. Thus, a young person who normally enjoys a high level of bodily health will react very quickly to a build-up of toxic waste in his tissues by producing a high fever accompanied by all the other symptoms of acute illness. Perspiration will be profuse, there may be a skin rash, diarrhoea, loss of appetite and perhaps sickness – all of which are clear manifestations of the body's eliminative and tissue-cleansing efforts operating at maximum efficiency.

In the space of a few days these emergency measures will have completed their task and the patient will be ready and eager to resume normal activities.

The innate vital forces which the body

mobilizes in order to safeguard its tissues and maintain the biochemic equilibrium which is essential to health and survival continue to operate these safety-valves in the form of acute illness throughout the formative years and into adulthood. They can, however, be gradually drained and depleted if, through ignorance or misguided counselling, an individual fails to appreciate their constructive purpose and consistently suppresses the body's waste-disposal efforts, while at the same time perpetuating the errors of omission and commission which have created the conditions which triggered off the emergency measures.

The human body has vast resources of vital energy, but with the passage of time the demands made upon them in an endeavour to deal with recurring bouts of acute illness take an increasing toll. Gradually, as its batteries become drained, the body is no longer able to react as vigorously to the repeated demands that are made upon it, and the safety-valves which have operated in the form of colds, influenza, etc. are employed less frequently.

Consequently, the toxic wastes which the body has struggled in vain to eliminate are forced ever more deeply into the system, involving such important organs as the stomach, the lungs, the liver, the bladder, the pancreas, the gall-bladder and the intestines, the functions of which become disorganized and progressively less efficient.

With the passage of years the suppressed catarrhal inflammation regresses into chronic catarrhal congestion, resulting in the pain and misery which are the hall-mark of such conditions as bronchitis, colitis, jaundice, gastritis, gall-stones and cystitis.

By the time these stages have been reached the impotence of orthodox medical treatment will have become all too apparent, and the unfortunate patient is likely to be faced with no alternative but to submit to radical surgery.

By this time, also, the patient and his medical advisers will long since have lost sight of the seemingly simple origins of the problems which have brought about this sorry state of affairs – the colds, coughs and other acute catarrhal illnesses which, many years earlier, should have been recognized as a warning that the body's complex but usually very efficient protective and regulating mechanisms were having difficulty in maintaining the delicate metabolic balance which alone can afford immunity from disease.

Our next task, therefore, is to retrace our steps and offer what we consider to be a more logical alternative to the orthodox view that germs and viruses are primarily responsible for the acute ailments which are the precursors of the chronic catarrhal disorders which plague so many people in later life.

6.

The Primary Causes of Catarrh

It is an unfortunate fact of life that very few people give any serious thought to the miracles which are accomplished daily in order that their bodies may grow and function efficiently throughout the seventy years or so that is generally regarded as the normal life-span. Only when something goes wrong do most of us become aware of the complex and hard-working organs and systems which constitute the living body – the heart, the lungs, the digestive system, the brain, the liver and kidneys and the vast network of veins and arteries.

Through the media of books and television programmes we may acquire a modest appreciation of what some of these organs look like and where they are located in the body, but many years of meticulous work by anatomists, biologists, physiologists and various other research scientists have succeeded only in unravelling relatively few of the mysteries which enable us to think, breathe, move and carry out the vast range of activities of which the living body is capable. Indeed, there is good reason to suspect that as the experts get to know more and more about the minutiae of the human organism they lose sight of the fact that the body is an *integration* of a fantastic array of component parts, and that it can only function efficiently *as a complete entity.*

The breakdown of any one organ implies a corresponding failure in the complex systems which are responsible for its maintenance. All too frequently, however, a doctor or surgeon who 'specializes' in a particular part of the human anatomy will concentrate all his efforts on the task of solving the specific problem, seemingly oblivious to the fact that his efforts in this direction are almost certain to prove abortive in the long term unless something is done to identify and deal with the possibly remote causes of the localized break-down.

To take a topical example, organ transplants are very much in the news today and an amazing degree of expertise is being developed in this field. Kidneys are replaced almost as a routine operation, and heart, lung and liver transplants are no longer regarded by the media as being particularly newsworthy unless the subject of the operation inspires some special emotive appeal.

Regrettably, however, although the operation itself is often acclaimed as having been 'successful', it is only very rarely that the patient's life is extended for any appreciable length of time, during which period he or she will be dependent upon constant medical supervision and the use of powerful drugs to prevent rejection of the 'foreign' organ.

The fact that 'the operation was successful but the patient died' is an all-too-frequent epitaph in these cases surely exemplifies the futility of the orthodox profession's policy of 'fighting' diseases with dangerous drugs and the scalpel – of concerning themselves only with the suppression of local symptoms or the removal of damaged components instead of seeking out and remedying the primary causes of systemic failure and organic breakdown.

We have already digressed briefly from our subject – catarrh – in order to impress upon the reader once again the need to look beyond the nose, or throat, or lungs or any other focal point in our search for the causes of catarrh, no matter how it may manifest itself or what organ is affected.

Congestion and inflammation of the mucous membranes and the accompanying excessive secretion of mucus is not a localized problem. It is an indication that the metabolic balance of the entire system has been disturbed and that the body is being forced to employ abnormal measures in an attempt to restore normal equilibrium.

What, then, *are* these primary causes of

catarrh to which we have referred so insistently in the preceding pages?

Without doubt faulty nutrition is by far the most frequent influence in regard not only to catarrh but many other common ailments. If we consider the matter objectively, it is not difficult to understand why this should be so for it is surely self-evident that the quality of any product is proportional to the quality of the materials employed in its manufacture. Surely, therefore raw food in its natural state, with its vitamin and mineral content still intact is the logical diet for the human body.

This may well have been the case in the distant past and even up to a century or so ago – until, that is, the time of the industrial revolution which drew vast numbers of people from the farms and villages into the cities and triggered off a radical change not only in the methods of food production but in the feeding habits of the people themselves.

In succeeding years the populations of most of the industrialized nations have multiplied on a prodigious scale, and in response to the demands of increasing numbers of city-dwellers the manufacturer took over the main role of food producer from the farmer. The latter continued to provide much of the raw material, but the end-products which emerged eventually from the factory bore little or no resemblance to the produce grown by the farmer.

Few items of our daily diet have suffered

more at the hands of the commercial processors than the bread which for centuries has been one of the staple foods in European communities.

Throughout the middle ages flour was produced in wind- or water-mills by grinding the wheat between special stones. The end-product tended to be coarse-grained but of a high extraction-rate, which means that it contained all the constituent parts of the wheat – not only the endosperm which makes up the starchy bulk of the grain, but also the germ and the outer husk or bran. Because the latter came through the milling process in the form of very fine scales it could be sifted out from the flour which could then be baked to provide a somewhat whiter loaf. This was, however, a complicated and expensive process and so only a few wealthy households were able to indulge themselves with what therefore became something of a status symbol.

It was not until well into the eighteenth century that technical developments began to bring about a transition from wind- and water-mills to steam-powered machinery, and also during this period the expansion in dairy farming, stemming from the increased demand for food from the larger urban populations, encouraged the millers to improve the sifting processes so that the bran could be sold to provide fodder for the cattle.

As a consequence, white flour could be produced more cheaply, leading to an increased demand for the 'status symbol' white loaf.

Towards the end of the eighteenth century even more important technical changes came about, resulting in the displacement of the flat millstones in favour of steel rollers and the use of special silk materials through which a very fine white flour could be sifted. By varying the speeds and surface-patterns of a succession of rollers it became possible to control to very fine limits the size of the flour-grain extracted at various stages of the milling process, which meant that ultimately all the bran and wheat-germ could be removed leaving only 70% or so of the original wheat-grain in the form of the pure white starchy endosperm.

From then on into the twentieth century white flour and white bread were consumed almost universally, while the millers were able to increase their profits by selling much of the extracted 30% for animal feeding purposes in the form of what have been marketed under such names as millers' offal, middlings, sharps and toppings.

The effect on the nutritional value of the whitest of white loaves can only be appreciated when we realize that the 70% · endosperm portion of the wheat which is used for bread-making consists of 84% starch and 12% protein, but only 2% fibre, 1.2% fat and approximately 0.45% minerals, whereas the remaining 30% which is extracted during the milling process – i.e. the bran and the wheat-germ – consists of 55.5% starch and 24.5% protein, and 7.25% fibre, 7.5% fat and 5.25% minerals.

As these figures show, the low-extraction-rate white flour will contain a considerably higher proportion of starch, but a substantially reduced ratio of protein and virtually no fibre, fat or minerals.

There are also considerable losses of the various vitamins of the B complex.

Dr Graham in the USA and Dr Allinson in the UK were probably the first nutritionists to recognize the serious health implications of the increasing public dependence on white bread and they are both immortalized through the wholewheat loaves which bear their names.

Graham, in the early years of the nineteenth century, and Allinson some fifty years later, both campaigned assiduously for the return of a high-extraction loaf, but in their times there were no scientific means of supporting their ideas which were consequently dismissed by the medical and health establishment as the groundless theories of over-enthusiastic cranks.

It was only when vitamins were discovered that it became possible to produce conclusive proof that wholemeal bread was indeed superior nutritionally to the popular pallid white loaf. This fact was demonstrated quite clearly in experiments on animals, and it was not long before unmistakable evidence was forthcoming to show that the nutritional deficiencies of white bread were largely responsible for certain types of human ailments.

During the First World War, in 1915, British troops in Mesopotamia were being struck down with beriberi – a disease which occurs as a direct result of a deficiency of vitamin B_1 and which has also become widespread in tropical countries since polished white rice was introduced as a staple dietary component in place of natural brown rice.

Vitamin B_1 (thiamine) is one of the constituents of the vitamin B complex which is seriously depleted during the milling and refining processes to which wholewheat is subjected in order to produce white flour. Indeed, 70% extraction flour contains only one-fifth of the original vitamin B_1 content of wholewheat flour.

Although the nutritional shortcomings of refined white flour and white bread were widely recognized, no official action was taken to improve the standards of commercial milling practice until the heavy shipping losses during the Second World War forced the Government to introduce what was known as National flour with an extraction rate of 85%.

This reform, however, was inspired not by a desire to safeguard public health but simply by the need to reduce the demands being made on a much depleted merchant fleet in transporting supplies of wheat to this country from North America. It took a crisis of this magnitude to bring home to officialdom the absurdity of putting ships and lives at risk to carry across the Atlantic thousands of tons of grain of which only 70% was to be used for human consumption.

Amazingly, however, the nutritional lessons had not been learned, and in the years following the end of the war the extraction rate was again allowed to fall progressively, and by the late nineteen-fifties all controls had been removed and the millers were free to provide flour of any extraction.

There was just one small concession to the nutritionists who had opposed this retrogressive step. Their case that low-extraction flour was seriously deficient in important nutrients was clearly incontrovertible, and so the legislators agreed reluctantly that all flour, with the exception of 100% wholemeal, should be 'fortified' with synthetic B vitamins (thiamine and nicotinic acid), iron and calcium carbonate (chalk). It should be noted, however, that these additives are pure chemicals, the nutritive values and metabolic effects of which differ very substantially from those of the original natural vitamins and minerals which are removed by the refining processes.

The depredations of the milling and baking industries are not confined to the manipulation of the nutritional components of their products. Over the years there has been a steady increase in the use of chemicals of various kinds, including bleaching agents, fat extenders, emulsifiers, improvers, stabilizing agents and anti-oxidants.

There is, it is always claimed, 'no evidence' that these substances are harmful to man, but the possibility must exist that any foreign chemical substance that is introduced into the living body, either alone or in combination with others, will have some detrimental effect on the complex and delicate chemical balance which is so vital to the health of that organism.

We have dealt at some considerable length with the nutritional implications of the commercial manipulation of flour and bread because these constitute what is undoubtedly one of the major dietary components among Western communities and because we maintain that an excessive consumption of refined starchy foods is one of the most frequent causes of catarrhal ailments.

Equally culpable, however, is cow's milk, the consumption of which has increased to an enormous extent throughout the twentieth century due to the extensive and highly efficient advertising campaigns which have been mounted by the marketing organizations.

It is true that milk has had a place in human dietetics throughout recorded history and that it has been used for this purpose in many parts of the world. A surprising variety of animals have been relied upon for its production by different nationalities, including cows, ewes, mares, goats, asses, reindeer and buffaloes.

There are, however, very considerable differences in the nutritive constituents of the milk derived from the various species, therefore it is totally fallacious to argue, as has so often been the case over the years, that because mother's milk is a perfect and complete food for a human baby, then the milk derived from very different creatures is necessarily an ideal food for human adults.

It is not even valid to claim that cow's milk is a satisfactory substitute for breast-milk as a food for infants, not only because of the nutritional differences (see Table 1, page 55) but also because of the qualitative changes which occur when milk is stored. For example, the fat in the milk taken by a baby straight from its mother's breast is in the form of very minute globules and in this form it is very easily digested. When milk is allowed to stand, however, the globules quickly coalesce to form cream, which can cause both digestive and assimilative problems for the infant.

Even when cow's milk is 'humanized' it is inevitable that subtle differences in the nature and chemical composition of its constituent parts will continue to modify its metabolic effects on the infant consumer, and it is widely recognized that breast-fed babies are substantially less likely to contract colds and other catarrhal infections than those reared on commercial baby-foods based on cow's milk and cereals.

Moreover, human milk has more carbohydrate, in the form of milk-sugar, than cow's milk, and when the latter is 'humanized' it is customary to add cane sugar or glucose. It is believed that this may explain why many infants become 'addicted' to unnaturally sweet foods at an early age, with dire consequences in later life in terms of dental decay, obesity and even diabetes.

Nutrients	Human Milk	Cow's Milk (Whole)
Protein	2.0g per 100g	3.4g per 100g
Carbohydrate	6.9g per 100g	4.8g per 100g
Fat	3.7g per 100g	3.7g per 100g
Vitamin A	170iu per 100g	125iu per 100g
Vitamin D	1.00iu per 100g	1.00iu per 100g
Vitamin B_1	0.17mg per 100g	0.04mg per 100g
Vitamin B_2	0.03mg per 100g	0.15mg per 100g
Vitamin C	3.50mg per 100g	2.00mg per 100g
Nicotinic Acid	3.50mg per 100g	0.08mg per 100g

Table 1. The main nutrients in human milk and cow's milk.

As is shown by the figures in Table 1, there is a very considerable difference in the amount of protein in human milk as compared with that in cow's milk – a fact which affords unmistakable evidence of the very different nutritional needs of human infants and calves.

If we bear in mind the fact that the latter grow and mature very much more quickly than human babies, it is significant that orthodox nutritionists have long recognized that children who are given ample quantities of cow's milk also tend to grow more rapidly and reach full maturity at an earlier age than those for whom milk has not made such a significant dietary contribution. Indeed, some of these authorities have questioned the desirability of this artificially induced growth-rate and have suggested that speeding up the rate of children's development may ultimately shorten their life-expectancy, as has been demonstrated by experiments on rats which were found to live longer when their diet was specifically controlled so as to postpone the onset of maturity.

Another factor which helps to support the view that cow's milk is basically unsuitable as a substitute for breast-milk was revealed by the discovery that the latter contains a nutrient substance which is essential for the development in the infant's bowel of a beneficial bacterium. This organism apparently creates an acid environment in the system which in turn is thought to promote the assimilation of the proteins in the milk. Cow's milk, on the other hand, does not contain this special nutrient, and it has been found that the bowels of artificially fed infants contain a number of very different bacteria the presence of which produces an alkaline or neutral environment.

Even more damning, perhaps, is the indisputable fact that cow's milk and the wheat proteins in bread constitute two of the most frequent causes of what are popularly known as food allergies – which are so often held to be responsible for such acute catarrhal reactions as asthma and hay-fever as well as eczema and certain types of digestive disorder.

An allergy, according to Professor Arnold Bender in his *Dictionary of Nutrition and Food Technology* (Butterworth's, London) is 'an altered or abnormal tissue reaction which may be caused by contact between a foreign protein, the allergen, and sensitive body tissues'. 'Food allergies,' he goes on to say, 'are more common in infants and the usual causes are eggs, milk and wheat ... The reactions may include nettle-rash, hay-fever, asthma and dyspepsia.'

In the context of our condemnation of cow's milk and white bread it is interesting that this very famous and highly qualified nutritionist attributes the responsibility for allergic reactions to 'contact with a *foreign protein*' while the compilers of medical reference books seem to be unanimous in citing milk and wheat as being two of the foods which most frequently trigger off allergic reactions.

In a sense, white flour and cow's milk may quite justifiably be regarded as 'foreign' substances since the former bears little resemblance to the natural wholewheat product and the latter was never intended to be a staple food for human infants – and certainly not for human adults.

And yet we are faced with a strange anomaly inasmuch as the vast majority of the millions of people who regularly consume these products are apparently immune to the so-called allergens which they are alleged to contain.

Surely, then, it is not the food itself which is the *primary* cause of hay-fever, asthma, eczema and the other 'allergies' which plague so many people today, but some systemic abnormality in the individual sufferers which renders them susceptible to irritants either in the foods themselves or in the atmosphere.

Here, again, the naturopathic philosophy provides a simple and logical explanation – namely, that the delicate metabolic balance in the patient's system has been disorganized as a result of consuming not only white bread and cow's milk but also a whole range of other commercially denatured foods and beverages. These products have been deprived of their original nutrients, cooked and manipulated through a series of complex factory processes and then 'fortified' with synthetic vitamins and minerals and treated with other chemical substances for the purpose of preserving, colouring, flavouring, emulsifying and thickening what remains of the original product in order to restore or increase its appeal to the customer's eye and palate and – even more important to the producer – to extend its shelf life and so enhance its profitability.

An investigation by the Consumers' Association journal *Which?* revealed that eight out of every ten packaged foods which they examined on the shelves of a supermarket contained additives of one sort or another. During the course of their survey they purchased 17 typical packaged food items from ten of the largest chainstores and found that the labels listed between 31 and 106 additives. The lowest scores were achieved by canned garden peas, salmon and shrimp paste and black cherry yogurt with minimum and maximum figures of 0 and 2, 1 and 2, and 0 and 3 additives respectively. At the top end of the scale they placed chocolate Swiss roll, with minimums and maximums of 5 and 13 additives, orangeades, tomato cup soup and beef sausages with 4 and 8, 3 and 9 and 4 and 8 respectively, vanilla ice-cream 2 and 8, soft margarines 3 and 6, and sweet pickles 2 and 7.

We have stressed previously that bodily health and natural immunity to disease are dependent upon the maintenance of the delicately balanced biochemical equilibrium which enables the complex systems to function efficiently. We have also pointed out that the raw materials which are used for this purpose *must* come from the food we eat, the beverages we drink and the air we breathe.

Is it surprising, then, that those who regularly

consume the types of products which constitute so much of the average housewife's food purchases should find that their abnormal chemical constituents trigger off an abnormal response in their tissues and organs?

Once again we would impress upon the reader that colds, coughs, sneezes and the other manifestations of catarrhal congestion and inflammation are *not* 'caught' and are not caused by germs, or viruses, or the so-called allergens. They represent a cry of distress from an abused and poisoned organism which is struggling to restore the metabolic equilibrium which alone can enable its complex organs and systems to function efficiently.

The mucous membranes, which in health carry out their protective and lubricating functions quietly and unobtrusively, are a part of the system of 'safety-valves' to be brought into service when the bowels, the kidneys, the lungs and the skin are unable to cope with the abnormal eliminative burdens imposed upon them.

Faulty nutrition, therefore, is the *primary* cause of catarrh, but there are other contributory factors as will be explained.

7.

Other Contributory Causes

Although nutritional imbalance has been indicted as the major causative factor in catarrhal disorders, the harmful effects of dietary excesses and deficiencies can be influenced in a variety of ways.

We have explained at some length the extent to which bodily health and natural immunity to disease are dependent upon the foods and beverages which we consume and the air we breathe, and it is the role of the latter which now needs to be considered.

Just as a healthy person remains totally unaware of the functions of digestion and assimilation which carry out the processes of dismantling the food we eat into the various chemical components needed for tissue maintenance and repair, so our lungs should continue to work with little or no conscious effort on our part and, in doing so, extract great quantities of oxygen from the inhaled air and then discharge carbon-dioxide into the atmosphere.

The fact that it is possible for us to survive for weeks or even months without food, and for days without water, but for only a few minutes without air is clearly indicative of the vital role which the lungs perform on our behalf, and it will be readily understood, therefore, that anything which impairs their efficiency may have very serious consequences in terms of bodily health.

Yet, through ignorance or thoughtlessness, there are many ways in which the respiratory organs can be abused, making them more susceptible to the damaging effects of catarrh. The reasons why this should be so will become clear when the mechanics of breathing and the ways in which the lungs perform their complex functions are explained.

The lungs themselves are not composed of muscular tissue and so the process of inspiration by means of which air is drawn in through the nose and mouth, down the windpipe (trachea) and into the lungs is accomplished by means of a co-ordinated series of actions of the rib-cage (thorax) and the diaphragm – a thin sheet of muscular tissue which forms the domed floor of the chest cavity. As will be seen in Figure 2 opposite, the thorax is enclosed by twelve pairs of ribs, all of which are attached at the rear to the spinal vertabrae, while the upper ten pairs are jointed, either directly or via a band of

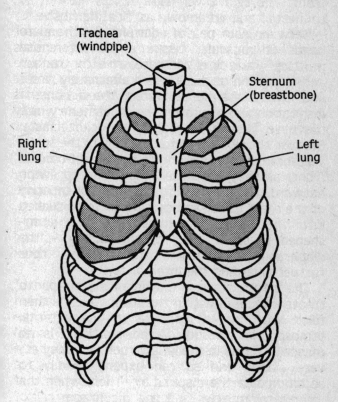

Figure 2.   The Thorax and lungs

strong cartilage, to the breast-bone (sternum) in front. The two lower pairs of ribs are not so connected and are known as 'floating ribs'.

Between each pair of adjacent ribs there are bands of muscular tissue – the intercostal muscles – and it is the successive contraction and relaxation of these which alternately raises and lowers the ribs to effect the actions of inspiration and expiration – a movement which has been likened to that of a bucket-handle. Because the ribs are jointed flexibly to the spinal vertebrae at the rear and to the breast-bone in front, as they are raised they tend to swing outward, thus increasing the internal capacity of the chest cavity and causing air to be sucked into the lungs. Simultaneously, the dome-shaped muscular floor of the thorax – the diaphragm – contracts and flattens, thus further enlarging the internal cavity.

The effect of these movements is simply to create a vacuum within the chest which is then filled with air in response to the external atmospheric pressure. Although there is no muscular tissue in the lung structures, they are very elastic and so can expand readily to accommodate the inspired air. Then, when the intercostal muscles and the diaphragm relax, thus reducing the thoracic capacity, the recoil of the elastic lung tissues forcibly expels the air through the nose and mouth.

Under normal conditions all these actions are carried out automatically, the rate of respiration being controlled by nervous impulses from the brain in order to meet the body's varying needs for oxygen, but, when necessary, it is possible for us to switch from 'automatic' to 'manual' control, so to speak, and the act of breathing can be consciously suspended or augmented – as for example, when swimming under water or blowing up a balloon.

As is shown in Figure 3 on page 66, air reaches the lungs via the trachea or windpipe which then divides to form the right and left bronchi, which in turn divide and sub-divide into tubes of ever-decreasing diameter. Finally, the smallest of these tubes open into minute elastic sacs which constitute the sponge-like tissues of the lungs in which their vital functions are carried out.

These tiny sacs (alveoli), of which there are hundreds of millions in each lung, are surrounded by masses of equally small blood-capillaries through the thin walls of which there is a constant interchange of gases – oxygen passing from the lungs into the blood-stream and carbon-dioxide being taken from the blood and expired through the nose and mouth.

In the context of the subject of this book, it is important to explain that the trachea and the many branches of the bronchial tubes are lined with mucous membranes from which a copious flow of mucus is secreted, the purpose of which is to trap particles of inhaled dust and other pollutants and prevent them from reaching the

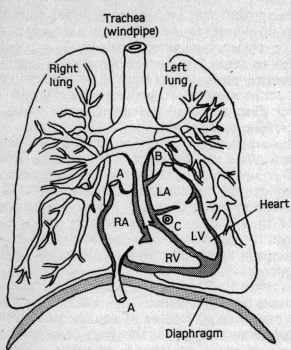

Figure 3. Heart and lung functions

Exhausted blood returns to right auricle (RA) at 'A', is passed into right ventricle (RV) then to the lungs, where carbon monoxide is unloaded and oxygen is taken up. It is then returned to the left auricle (LA) at 'B' via the pulmonary artery (not shown), passed into the left ventricle (LV) and carried around the body via the aorta 'C'.

lung tissues. The tiny hair-like cilia on the surface of the bronchial membranes (see Figure 1, p. 15) then sweep the dust-laden mucus back up to the throat to be swallowed or expectorated.

All of these ingenious processes are carried out continuously and efficiently under normal circumstances, but it is not difficult to envisage the problems that can arise if mucous glands become chronically inflamed and over-active.

Under these circumstances, the flow of mucus will be increased to such an extent that it can no longer be cleared from the air-passages which will gradually become obstructed and their tissues will degenerate and perhaps ulcerate. Eventually, the deeper tissues of the lungs will become involved, leading to dilatation of the tiny air-sacs and progressive impairment of the functional efficiency of the lungs.

This is largely because the capacity of the lungs to effect the necessary exchange of oxygen and carbon-dioxide in the very short interval between inhalation and exhalation is made possible by the enormous surface area of the millions of alveoli with which the inspired air comes into contact with each breath. Inevitably, when the alveoli become greatly distended as the result of chronic catarrhal congestion the effective area is seriously curtailed. The problem is further accentuated by the walls of the distended alveoli becoming increasingly thickened and fibrous tissue taking the place of the elastic fibres, thus reducing the ability of the lungs to contract and expire the carbon-dioxide saturated air. The end-result of this insidious process of lung tissue degeneration is the very serious and possibly fatal disease known as emphysema.

This condition represents the ultimate break-down in the vital role which the simple act of breathing plays in pumping oxygen into the bloodstream and removing some of the waste products of metabolism.

It is, however, the circulatory system which performs the equally vital task of transporting nutrients to the various tissues of the body and returning cell wastes and other unwanted and potentially harmful substances to the elimin-ative organs. Consequently, catarrh and any of the other ill-effects of faulty nutrition will be accentuated if the circulatory system is impaired, and this is a condition which is becoming increasingly prevalent for a variety of reasons.

Primarily, however, lack of physical exercise is undoubtedly responsible for almost as much illness as faulty nutrition, and these two factors together must bear an enormous burden of responsibility, not only for acute catarrhal maladies but also for the ever-increasing incidence of organic failure and degenerative disease.

Few people realize the extent to which the functional efficiency and physical strength of the heart, the blood-vessels, the liver, the lungs, the kidneys and other vital organs are dependent upon regular physical activity, and yet this fundamental biological truth becomes all too obvious when we understand the basic mechanics of the circulatory system.

Television programmes and articles in popular magazines and the newspapers devote a great deal of attention to the miracles of modern medicine, but it is probably true to say that the average layman knows more about open-heart surgery, organ transplants, hip-replacements, tumour excision and many other extraordinarily skilful feats of surgical wizardry than he does about the day-to-day workings of his own body.

Many, no doubt, are aware that blood is pumped by the heart through the arteries to all parts of the body and that it is then returned to the heart via a network of veins. That, however, is a gross over-simplification of the system upon which the infinitely complex organs and tissues of the human body depend for their maintenance and renewal over the 70-year period which constitutes the traditional individual life-span.

The heart is, of course, the muscular pump which provides the initial circulatory impetus, but in addition to supplying blood to fuel the muscles and maintain the various tissues and organs of the body, it is also responsible for pumping it to the lungs where, as we have explained earlier in this chapter, it discharges carbon-dioxide and is recharged with oxygen.

This dualling of the circulatory system is possible because the heart has four chambers operating as two separate pairs (see Figure 3, page 66). Freshly oxygenated blood from the lungs enters the upper of two chambers on the left side of the heart (the left auricle) which then contracts, forcing the fluid into the lower chamber (the left ventricle). The thick muscular walls of the latter then contract, propelling the blood through the arterial system to nourish the various parts of the body, then through a network of tiny capillaries and into the veins which carry it back to the heart where it enters the upper right-hand chamber (the right auricle). The contraction of the latter then sends the blood into the right ventricle from which it is pumped on the final stage of its journey – i.e. back to the lungs, where it discharges the carbon-dioxide collected during the course of its travels, takes up a fresh charge of oxygen and is returned once more to the left auricle.

It is estimated that a single drop of blood will accomplish the complete cycle – from the left ventricle, around the body, back to the right auricle, on to the lungs and finally back to the left auricle – in approximately 30 seconds. This is a remarkable achievement by any standards, but it is rendered even more so by reason of the fact that during its journey around the body a proportion of the blood-supply is diverted to the intestines where it takes up nutrients before passing on to the liver where it is purified and relieved of some of its food material before re-entering the general circulation en route back to the heart. At the same time, blood is diverted to the kidneys where more toxins are filtered out and excreted in the urine.

In order that this extraordinary and complex cycle of events may be carried out efficiently it is, of course, essential that the blood should flow freely throughout its long journey, and it is here that the need for regular exercise becomes imperative.

As we have explained, the heart provides an extremely efficient motivating force which impels the blood along the arterial network on the first stage of its circulatory tour of duty, but by the time it reaches the capillaries and crosses over into the veins most of this propulsive power has been dissipated, which poses a not inconsiderable problem, inasmuch as the large volume of blood circulating in the lower limbs and organs now has to overcome the efforts of gravity and be forced upward through the veins in order to complete the second stage, its passage back to the heart.

Nature has, of course, made adequate provision to cope with this situation. In the first place, the veins are provided with a series of valves which open to allow the blood to pass upward and then snap shut so as to prevent any reflux.

The primary mechanism which the body employs in order to overcome the forces of gravity and inertia in the veins of the lower limbs and abdomen is the rhythmic contraction and relaxation, during the course of vigorous physical exercise, of the powerful muscles which surround the blood-vessels. For example, when we perform the simple act of walking, the initial pressure on the front of the foot causes contraction of the calf-muscles, compressing the large veins embedded between them and forcing the blood up into the thigh where it is retained by the closure of the valves. As the leg swings forward the calf-muscles relax, allowing the veins to refill, while simultaneously the thigh muscles contract to take the weight of the body and again the blood is pumped on into the abdomen. Swinging the arms as we walk has a somewhat similar effect on the veins in the upper limbs.

The upward pressure produced by the 'muscle pump' continues to assist the blood-flow through the abdomen, reinforced, of course, by the contraction of the muscles of the buttocks and those of the pelvis, but at this stage a new propulsive mechanism is enlisted. The diaphragm which, as we have already observed, is largely responsible for efficient lung-function, serves as an equally useful circulatory aid. Stimulated by the increased demands for oxygen created by the muscular activity, the breathing becomes faster and deeper, as a result of which the diaphragm rises and falls more vigorously. As it contracts it compresses the contents of the abdomen which in turn squeeze the veins, forcing the blood up into the chest cavity and back into the heart. Then, as the diaphragm relaxes and rises, a partial vacuum is created in the abdomen which helps to draw a fresh consignment of blood up from the lower limbs.

It will be abundantly clear, however, that the efficiency of this ingenious circulatory system is dependent very largely on frequent and regular bodily activity. Unfortunately, since the early years of the twentieth century inventors and technologists have worked untiringly to ensure that the demands on man's physical resources shall be reduced to a minimum.

Thanks to the advances in private and public transport facilities we are no longer dependent on our legs for even relatively short trips to shops or to visit friends, and the television set now ensures that sports, films and other forms of entertainment are available 'on tap' as it were without, in many cases, the need to leave a comfortable armchair even to switch from one programme to another.

In recent years there has been a rapid increase in the incidence of degenerative diseases such as bronchitis, heart-failure and high blood-pressure which are now widely recognized as being due largely to physical inactivity and faulty nutrition, but with few exceptions neither the medical profession nor the general public appreciate the extent to which these same factors are implicated as major causative factors in the simple catarrhal ailments which all too often are the precursors of crippling and even fatal illnesses.

Nor are lack of exercise and the resultant circulatory and breathing defects the only penalties which we have to pay for the comforts afforded by the technological advances which have taken place at such a tremendous rate in comparatively recent years.

Closely allied to the circulatory system provided by the heart, arteries and veins is the lymphatic system, of the existence of which few people are aware, while even fewer appreciate the important functions which it serves both in nourishing the cells and neutralizing and removing the waste products of metabolism and potentially harmful bacteria.

Lymph is a thin, colourless liquid which is derived from the blood plasma. As the blood permeates through the capillaries prior to entering the veins and returning to the heart, some of it is filtered into the adjacent lymphatic capillaries carrying with it a variety of nutrient substances – e.g. oxygen, sugar, emulsified fats and protein – which are required by the tissue cells in order to maintain their vital functions.

These tiny capillaries – like those which link the arteries and veins – drain the lymph into progressively larger vessels, called lymphatics, which eventually combine to form two main trunks passing upward through the chest, where they are joined by lymphatics from the thorax and arms, and then open into two large veins in the neck so that the lymph is returned to the general circulatory system from which it was originally drawn.

In the course of its passage from the capillaries and back to the veins, the lymph passes through a series of glands which are situated at strategic points throughout the entire body, and which serve as filters to remove harmful bacteria and toxic substances. They also produce masses of specialized white blood corpuscles – called leucocytes – which attack and 'digest' the harmful organisms and toxins so that the lymph fluid is cleansed and purified before it re-enters the bloodstream.

The vital protective functions which are thus performed by the lymphatic system are exemplified by a phenomenon with which most of us are quite familiar – i.e. the swollen glands which become readily palpable in the neck when the throat or tonsils become infected, or those in the armpits which become enlarged and hard when injury to the hand becomes septic or when a boil erupts on the limb.

The lymphatics can, however, carry out their important functions effectively only when, like the blood, the lymph can circulate freely through the ducts and glands and here, again, the efficiency of the system is very largely dependent upon the propulsive support of the 'muscle pump'.

Regular physical exercise is therefore trebly important, firstly, to stimulate deep breathing and so ensure that the blood is adequately supplied with oxygen in exchange for carbon-dioxide; secondly to maintain an efficient circulation and so supply essential nutrients to all the organs and tissues of the body and remove cell wastes; and thirdly to ensure that the lymph can circulate freely through the glands which play such a vital part in maintaining natural immunity from disease.

Before concluding our review of the various contributory causes of catarrhal maladies we must refer briefly to the harmful effects of faulty posture, inadequate ventilation and the misguided choice of clothing.

Because we have already dealt at some length with the influence of the lungs and circulatory system on bodily health in general and catarrh in particular, it should not be difficult for the reader to appreciate that the functional efficiency of these vital organs can be quite seriously impaired by postural defects. Any tendency to adopt a stooping attitude when standing or walking, or to spend lengthy periods sitting slumped over a desk or work-bench, or in an armchair reading or watching television, will inevitably inhibit the actions of the ribs and dia-phragm and cause compression and congestion in the abdomen, with dire consequences in terms of both respiration and circulation.

These functions will be further impaired by poor ventilation in the home or place of employment, particularly if the air is fouled by dust, tobacco smoke or other pollutants.

It is surely not necessary to stress the very serious health consequences to which cigarette-smokers expose themselves, and it must be self-evident that very determined efforts must be made to break this very harmful and anti-social habit before there can be any real hope of eradicating catarrh and averting the greater risks of disabling diseases such as bronchitis and emphysema and ultimately of cancer of the lips, throat and lungs.

Finally, and again very briefly, mention must be made of the ways in which our choice of clothing can influence our susceptibility to colds, coughs and catarrh.

As we have mentioned earlier, the skin not only provides a strong protective covering for the body but is also one of its main excretory and eliminative organs, besides housing the vital sensory nerves which enable us to discriminate between harmful and beneficial environmental characteristics and take appropriate precautions in response to the dangers implicit in sensations of pain, heat and cold.

It follows, therefore, that anything which interferes with these functions poses some degree of threat to bodily welfare, and it is a strange paradox that intelligent Man is the only living organism which deliberately sets out to thwart Nature by coddling his body in a protective cocoon of clothing.

Since one of Nature's laws decrees that 'what

we do not use, we lose', it is perhaps reasonable to assume that at some stage of the evolutionary process Man lost the protective covering of hair with which other quadrupeds in temperate climates are equipped, because he took to covering his body with the skins and fur of the animals which he hunted and killed. Over the years he has progressively 'improved' on the measures which he has employed to render obsolete the very efficient thermostatic equipment which enables the body to adapt to a remarkably wide range of temperature variations.

Primarily, this is achieved by a combination of two ingenious mechanisms. In cold weather, the capillaries just beneath the skin contract, forcing the blood deep into the body so that it cannot be cooled by exposure to the surrounding air. Conversely, in hot weather the same blood-vessels dilate, drawing blood to the surface where, provided that the external temperature is below that of the body – i.e. 37°C or 98.6°F – it is cooled before continuing its tour of duty.

When the body is exposed to very high temperatures, or when abnormal heat is generated by vigorous physical exercise, it enlists the aid of the sweat-glands to supplement the cooling effects of the circulatory 'radiator', since the evaporation of profuse perspiration on the skin has a cooling effect on the underlying tissues and the blood that is drawn to the surface in response to the dilatation of the capillaries.

The excretory functions of the skin make a very important contribution to the body's eliminative capacity, and it has been estimated that the average adult exudes only slightly less than one litre ($1\frac{3}{4}$ pints) of perspiration in 24 hours, although most of this is given off in the form of invisible vapour. Dissolved in this sweat are a variety of organic residues including quite large amounts of sodium chloride (salt) and sodium phosphate, as well as sulphur and fatty acids.

The physiological value of the skin as an eliminative organ is demonstrated by the remarkable fact that in cases of acute kidney failure the sweat glands can be stimulated to take over a major part of their excretory functions, allowing the damaged organs to be rested and repaired.

From what has been said, therefore, it will we hope be apparent that when we cocoon our bodies in what are often poorly ventilated and non-absorbent materials, such as nylon and other synthetic fabrics, we not only disorientate the nervous, glandular and metabolic systems which are responsible for maintaining a stable body temperature, but also subdue an important component of the 'safety-valve' system.

Thus the body's attempts to eliminate toxic

waste materials released into the tissues from denatured and chemically manipulated food products are thwarted at every turn. The functions of the overloaded bowels, kidneys and liver are impaired, the skin cannot function as an emergency outlet, and when the body seeks, as a last resort, to get rid of the poisons through the mucous membranes this escape route is also blocked by suppressive medication.

If we appear to have devoted an inordinate amount of space to explanations of the many things which, in the past, the sufferer from catarrh may have done or left undone it is because ideas and customs which have been deeply ingrained in our minds for a lifetime are not easily changed or dislodged. If, therefore, the effects of mistaken or misguided actions are to be corrected it is essential that there shall be a clear understanding not only of *what* needs to be done but *why* each stage of the treatment programme must be carried out conscientiously.

Armed with this knowledge, the reader will be able to appreciate the logic of what he or she is required to do, or not do. What is equally important is that he or she will understand the nature and significance of the functional and physical changes which are likely to be experienced as the body responds to a series of measures which, perhaps, for the first time in many years, are actively promoting its long-suppressed capacity for self-healing instead of thwarting it.

Once it is accepted that catarrh is not a disease but simply a normal protective response to abnormal internal and external conditions which threaten its vital functions, the way is cleared for a positive and objective approach to the problems of restoring the metabolic equilibrium which alone can make it possible to 'cure' catarrh.

8.

The First Priority

In our review of the primary and contributory causes of catarrh we indicted white flour and its many commercial derivatives as public health enemy number one.

There is encouraging evidence that this view – which naturopaths and those who were derided as 'food cranks' have proclaimed for at least a century – is at last being accepted by orthodox medical practitioners and nutritionists, although not without a substantial amount of pressure from an increasingly enlightened section of the general public.

Until well into the middle of the twentieth century the 'experts' who largely dictated medical thinking in this country were insisting that dietetic habits had little or no influence in terms of human health and disease, and any suggestion from a patient that a change of diet might be beneficial was almost invariably dismissed out of hand.

The first signs of a change of medical attitudes came with the grudging admission that some increasingly common bowel disorders – e.g. constipation, colitis and diverticulitis – were caused primarily by a diet containing a high proportion of refined white-flour foods such as white bread, white rice and pasta, and processed breakfast cereals, all of which are virtually devoid of the natural fibre which, as naturopaths have always insisted, are essential to the functional efficiency of the human bowel and digestive system.

The extent of this revolution in orthodox medical thinking can only be appreciated when it is remembered that prior to this belated 'discovery' it was almost invariably the practice to advise patients suffering from colitis and diverticulitis to avoid all fibrous foods and have a bland, low-residue diet – the very foods which are now accepted as being mainly responsible for the serious functional breakdown.

It is, however, typical of the fragmentary thinking of the medical establishment that they now saw dietary fibre as a specific remedy rather than as an integral component of a healthful, wholefood diet, and patients were 'prescribed' comparatively large quantities of bran as a supplement to their normal meals.

They have yet to accept the naturopathic concept that the human body functions as a co-ordinated entity, the organs and systems of which can be maintained in full health and efficiency only if they are provided with the proper raw materials in the form of whole foods which contain such nutrients as vitamins, minerals, proteins and fats, as well as fibre, *in their natural form and combinations.*

Any attempt by the 'experts' to juggle with these components, whether by concentration, extraction or dilution, inevitably poses potentially serious metabolic problems for the consumer which eventually will result in some degree of organic or systemic disturbance.

As we have stressed in a previous chapter, white bread and the many other white-flour derivatives represent the ultimate in the commercial manipulation and exploitation of a staple food which has been transformed from a wholesome, natural raw material – the wheat grain – into a conglomeration of very unnatural products from the chemical laboratory combined with what is left after the millers have removed the bran and the most nutritious part of the wheat-grain – the wheat-germ – both of which are then packaged and sold to the public at high prices as 'nutritional supplements'!

White bread is only one – though certainly the worst – example of the denatured foods which constitute far too large a part of the present-day diet of vast numbers of people in Western communities, and which insidiously, over a period of many years perhaps, has been responsible for the nutritional defects which disorganize body chemistry and overwhelm its tissue-repairing and self-healing facilities.

Those who have read and understood all that has been said in the preceding chapters concerning the nature of acute and chronic catarrhal diseases and the significance and causes of their symptoms will readily appreciate why the first priority in any rational treatment programme must be to review our past and present dietary habits, identify the errors of omission and commission, and then put into effect whatever changes may be necessary to restore metabolic equilibrium and reactivate the body's self-healing resources.

It will be appreciated, however, that the very fact that a catarrhal problem exists is a clear indication that the eliminative system is under stress and that, as a result, the tissue cells and fluids are overburdened with toxic residues which must be disposed of as a preliminary to rebuilding them and restoring them to their full functional efficiency.

For this purpose it is necessary to undertake what amounts to a thorough physiological 'spring-clean', confining the diet to what are regarded, in naturopathic terms, as the cleansing or detoxifying foods – the fruits, vegetables and salads which are a bountiful source of a variety of vitamins as well as providing a goodly proportion of pure liquid and sufficient fibre to motivate the digestive system and stimulate bowel function.

Initially, however, it is necessary to rest the digestive tract and reduce any acidity by taking alkaline liquids only – e.g. dilute fruit or vegetable juices or home-made vegetable soup, together with non-acid fruits.

This preliminary regimen will be continued for three days, during which time it is possible that the newly stimulated eliminative processes which will be set in motion may induce some of the symptoms which, as we have already explained, are indicative that the body's self-healing functions are being mobilized in order to rid the tissues of toxic substances.

A feeling of being generally 'out of sorts', or the onset of a cold, sore throat, headache or coated tongue should, therefore, be welcomed as a sure sign that the desired tissue-cleansing procedures are already beginning to operate. In order to increase their effectiveness it is a good plan to take a moderately hot Epsom salts bath (see Appendix C, page 118), then retire to bed immediately in a darkened but well-ventilated room, and sleep for as long as possible.

On rising, the whole body should be sponged down or sprayed with cold or luke-warm water and then dried briskly with a coarse towel in order to stimulate elimination via the skin and tone up the surface capillaries.

During the next four days fresh fruit and frequent drinks of dilute juices, soup or water will still be taken and, in addition, a mixed vegetable salad and steamed green or root vegetables.

The diet will be further amplified during the second week of the cleansing programme. Only fruit and fruit or vegetable juice will be taken at breakfast time, and the midday meal will consist of a salad with one or two slices of wholewheat bread or toast, or crispbread, and the evening meal will consist of steamed vegetables and fresh fruit, preceded if desired by a bowl of vegetable soup.

At this stage the cleansing process should be well advanced, and the diet for the third week is intended to prepare the digestive tract for a balanced diet of simple whole foods (for more details see the Self-Cleansing Programme on page 107).

It is likely that in the early stages of the spring-clean regime the sudden and drastic departure from 'normal' feeding habits may be reflected in sluggish bowel function, and to guard against this eventuality it may be desirable to take on rising each morning a tumbler of one of the proprietary mineral waters which are now widely available.

In those cases where constipation has proved a problem a mild herbal laxative, obtainable from health food stores, may be taken from time to time as necessary, but care should be taken to avoid routine dependence on what should be regarded as a short-term supportive measure, and the bowel should be given every encouragement to function normally in response to the natural stimulus afforded by the dietary fibre.

Those who have embarked on this course of

treatment confident that they can at last look forward to a future free from the misery of catarrh are unlikely to have any difficulty in completing the preliminary cleansing regime, and it is hoped that they will be encouraged to go into the next stage of consolidation with the same degree of enthusiasm.

It must be remembered that persistent catarrh constitutes a deep-seated metabolic disturbance which has developed slowly, often over a period of many years, as a result of a variety of causative factors, and it would be unrealistic therefore to expect to repair damaged tissues and restore defective functions in the space of a few weeks or without a degree of patience and perseverance.

In any attempt to regain lost health the rewards are inevitably proportional to the effort and dedication that are brought to the task. This little homily is delivered because once the preliminary and relatively short cleansing regime has been completed it is necessary to embark on a long-term programme of rebuilding and revitalizing measures. In most cases this necessitates making what initially may seem to be quite drastic changes in one's diet and life-style, and this will most certainly mean breaking old and deeply ingrained habits many of which will have had their origins in infancy.

Man, like most other animals, is a creature of habit, and few people realize the extent to which their lives are governed by social, racial and national customs and conventions. They go to bed at more or less the same time each day, get up in the morning, carry out the ritual preliminaries of washing and dressing almost without conscious thought, eat a hurried breakfast and then set about a programme of pre-ordained activities interspersed at appropriate intervals with tea or coffee breaks and meals.

The types of food they eat are, perhaps, dictated almost exclusively by habit, and what is termed 'an acquired taste' due to long-term habituation can produce some strange and often bizarre differences in dietetic preferences not merely between one race or nationalilty and another but even between not very distant regions in the same country.

Few British people would relish such exotic delicacies as lark's tongues or bird's-nest soup, nor the snails or frogs legs which our near neighbours just across the Channel consume with such relish.

Even in this country, what is regarded as a traditional dish in one region is rejected as distasteful in another, and the extent to which many people are ruled by their feeding habits is exemplified by the fact that in countries such as France and Spain, on which vast numbers of British holiday-makers converge every year, a considerable catering industry has grown up to meet the demands of those who refuse to touch the local dishes and insist on having the fish and chips, sausages and chips, etc. to which they are accustomed at home.

Inevitably, therefore, a not inconsiderable effort of will may be called for in order to effect the necessary changes from the diet of denatured, conventional foods which are largely responsible for catarrh and other systemic disorders, in favour of the simple whole foods which retain the essential nutrients and form the basis on which we can rebuild damaged tissues and organs and restore their functional efficiency.

Given the necessary incentive, however, it is possible to break even the most deeply ingrained habit patterns, and there can surely be no more desirable reward for whatever short-term sacrifice may be called for than the knowledge that health *can* be regained and that in a surprisingly short time the new and different habits will become as firmly established as the old ones which they have replaced.

It has been made abundantly clear in earlier chapters that white bread and milk are the catarrh sufferer's worst dietetic enemies, and these, therefore must be the first targets for reform, along with the other white-flour and milk concoctions such as cakes, pastries, biscuits, white rice and pastas, sweetened breakfast cereals and, of course, milk foods and beverages.

Special emphasis must be placed on

commercial breakfast cereals because of their very great popularity as a cheap and easily prepared breakfast dish. The combination of refined starch, cow's milk and white sugar constitutes a very considerable hazard for anyone who is subject to catarrhal disorder, and there is little doubt that the increasing popularity of this product among children – amounting almost to addiction in some cases – must bear a considerable share of responsibility for the very high incidence of colds, tonsillitis and similar acute illnesses in young people.

Fortunately, the adoption of wholewheat bread, crispbread, muesli and other wholegrain cereal products in place of the refined white varieties usually presents few transitionary problems. The palate adjusts very quickly to the differences in taste and texture and most people find that within a week or two they no longer crave the insipid and woolly-textured white-flour product.

At this stage, however, it is necessary to remind readers of the over-riding importance of *balanced* nutrition, and the fact that an excess of starchy foods, no matter from what source they are derived, can well impair progress towards better health.

Individual nutritional needs can vary very considerably from one person to another, and even in the same person from one day to the next, depending upon such factors as physical activities, age, general health, occupation, and changing weather conditions, but a general principle which most naturopaths accept is that a balanced diet should consist of approximately 20% of the starchy and sugary carbohydrate foods, 20% proteins, and the remaining 60% of the vitamin-rich 'cleansing' fruits, vegetables and salads.

In Appendix D on page 119 we set out specimen menus to illustrate how this balance can be achieved and, we hope, demonstrate that the adoption of a health-promoting, wholefood diet need not entail costly and revolutionary changes in the family's catering arrangements.

Indeed, the most significant variation from what, for want of a better term, we will call 'normal' household shopping practice will be a reduction in the purchases of often expensive packeted and processed convenience foods and a corresponding increase in fresh produce from the greengrocer.

A little less bread may be needed, of a different colour and consistency of course, and what little milk may be needed for culinary uses and the occasional cup of tea or decaffeinated coffee – preferably unsweetened – could perhaps be of the skimmed or half-skimmed variety. Here, again, the taste-buds may need some initial coaxing to accept the modified flavour, but since such small quantities are involved, the continued indulgence of full milk will have little effect on the overall dietary balance.

For most families, the main meal of the day will remain virtually unchanged, inasmuch as it will consist basically of a protein dish accompanied either by green and root vegetables or occasionally a mixed salad incorporating a protein element. Whether the latter consists of meat or fish, or a cheese or egg dish, or a vegetarian savoury based on nuts or soya, is not very important, but fried or fatty meats should be avoided.

As with cereal foods, moderation should be observed in regard to protein consumption. These foods are the body's main source of the twenty amino-acids, which are the materials from which all living tissue cells are constructed and maintained. Twelve of these can be synthesized within the body, but the remaining eight – termed essential amino-acids – *must* be provided in the diet, and since the number and combination of these nutrients differs from one protein source to another, variety is just as important as quantity in this respect.

At this stage it is relevant to stress the need to adopt methods of cooking which will minimize the loss of nutrients, particularly where vegetables and fruits are concerned, because the vitamins and minerals of which these foods are such a valuable source can easily be destroyed by excessive heat, or by leaching when foods are boiled in water which is then thrown away.

To minimize these losses, what are termed

conservative cooking methods should be employed whenever possible – i.e. braising or steaming, or using only a small amount of water which is then utilized to make gravy or soup.

The use of a pressure-cooker is also permissible provided that the recommended cooking times are adhered to *meticulously*. Because of the very high temperatures involved with this type of cooking even a small error in the timing can cause a disproportionate amount of damage to some of the heat-sensitive vitamins, especially ascorbic acid (vitamin C). The guiding principles in regard to conservative cooking are minimum time, minimum heat and minimum use of water.

This, of course, underlines the value of raw fruits and vegetables, nuts and uncooked sprouted grains as an integral part of a whole-food diet, particularly when compost-grown produce is obtainable fresh from a reliable source. Those, however, who have been accustomed to having little or no raw food will need to exercise some caution in regard to the extent to which they introduce uncooked vegetables and salads into their diet, in order to allow their digestive systems to adapt to the new demands and problems thus imposed upon them.

In these cases it is wise to make the dietary changes slowly over a period of two or three months, starting with small salad meals, which are eaten slowly and masticated thoroughly, and gradually increasing the quantity and variety of raw produce, depending upon the degree of digestive tolerance.

Understandably, special masticatory problems will be experienced by older people with poor teeth or ill-fitting dentures, who will probably need to rely largely on conservatively cooked vegetables and stewed or soaked fresh or dried fruits, except for the softer items such as ripe pears, melon, oranges, etc.

In all cases, however, only fully ripened produce should be included in the diet.

The three-weeks' spring-cleaning programme followed by the adoption of a balanced dietary regime will, in all but the most chronic and deep-seated catarrhal conditions, have cleared the system of toxic debris and restored metabolic equilibrium so that the mucous membranes will no longer be called upon to supplement the body's main eliminative organs.

As we have pointed out, however, the health and functional efficiency of the individual systems and organs can only be ensured if the body *as a whole* is properly maintained in good working order, and our next priority, therefore, will be to explain the other therapeutic measures which need to be adopted to ensure that the benefits already secured are maintained.

9.

Restoring Natural Immunity

In Chapter 4 we explained that, contrary to orthodox teaching, germs, viruses and other micro-organisms – including, no doubt, many that have not yet been detected by research scientists even with the aid of their most sophisticated electronic equipment – play a constructive role in the natural order of the living world. At best, they perform complex chemical processes, neutralizing potentially harmful substances within the body and synthesizing vitamins and other essential nutrients which would otherwise not be available to us. At worst, they are scavengers which prey upon dead and decaying matter, digesting and eliminating it so that its basic mineral and other tissue components can be utilized to the benefit of other living creatures.

In order that we may live in harmony with these organisms the one essential is that we shall maintain a satisfactory level of natural immunity – i.e. a condition in which all our organs and systems are functioning efficiently, absorbing the essential nutrients from wholesome foods and beverages, and excreting the unwanted residues. This, in short, is the condition which we term *health*, which in turn means *wholeness*. It is the condition in which the beneficial bacteria can thrive and work on our behalf, but which deprives the so-called 'harmful' germs and viruses of the toxic substances which enable them to multiply.

We have taken the first step towards achieving this elusive goal when we have understood that the food we eat *must* be of a quality and nature which will provide the body with the raw materials which it requires for tissue maintenance and repair. Our next priority is to ensure that the circulatory, respiratory, assimilative, eliminative and other systems are able to perform their various tasks efficiently so that the oxygen, vitamins, minerals, amino-acids and other complex nutrients are made available for use as and where they are needed.

If, therefore, our first priority has been achieved and a balanced whole-food diet has been adopted, we must now take steps to improve the efficiency of the lungs, the heart and the circulatory system which, as we have stressed, have all too often been allowed to stagnate as a result of a sedentary life-style.

What is needed, therefore, is some form of physical exercise which can be indulged in by all reasonably able-bodied people and which does not entail the use of complex and costly gadgets and equipment.

The simple and supremely natural activity which fulfils all these requirements is, of course, walking, which bestows a very wide range of physiological benefits in return for little more than a modicum of self-discipline and perhaps some adjustment of daily time-tables and commitments.

Initially, the aim should be to take a brisk walk of half an hour or so at least once daily, which can often be fitted into the normal domestic or occupational schedule simply by leaving the car in the garage and walking to the shops, station or place of employment. Alternatively, the car can be parked a mile or so from one's destination and then completing the journey on foot.

To maximize the benefit derived from this exercise it is only necessary to move as briskly as one's physical capacity permits, swing the arms, hold the head high, straighten the spine and breathe deeply. The effects of this simple combination of physical and postural precautions is surprisingly extensive: the muscles of the legs, thighs, arms and shoulders pump the blood vigorously through the network of veins back into the thorax and then to the heart; deep breathing sends streams of oxygen-enriched air into the deeper recesses of the lungs which are seldom reached under normal conditions; the increased activity of the diaphragm not only supplements the blood-flow effected by the 'muscle-pump' but also 'massages' the stomach and intestines and so encourages peristalsis; the postural adjustments straighten the neck and spinal column thus taking pressure off the nerve trunks emerging from the spinal cord; finally, vigorous activity stimulates and strengthens a vast range of muscles, including those of the heart and other vital organs.

All this can be achieved with great economy of physical effort and in return for a modest adjustment of the daily timetable which, for many people such as housewives, the self-employed and older retired people can be achieved with little or no disruption of normal routine.

Complementary to the role of exercise is that of clothing and its effects on the efficiency of the skin as a protective and excretory organ. These vital functions can only be performed effectively if they are allowed to do so, and yet all too often civilized man appears to set out deliberately to thwart Nature's efforts to safeguard his health and his life.

In few ways, perhaps, is this more clearly exemplified than by our choice of clothing and the types of material from which it is made.

We have already explained that the skin is very largely responsible for the maintenance of a stable body temperature, and that this is achieved largely by two ingenious mechanisms –

the dilatation or contraction of the surface blood-vessels and the activities of the sweat-glands.

Both of these systems are almost completely frustrated if the body is enveloped in materials which are both non-absorbent and impervious to the passage of air, such as is the case with many of the modern synthetic fabrics like nylon.

It is estimated that even when the body is at rest approximately one pint of perspiration will be excreted daily, and that in hot weather, or under conditions of high atmospheric humidity, or as a result of strenuous physical activity, the same quantity may be lost in no more than an hour.

It is essential, therefore, that all clothing, but especially underwear, should be made of cotton or wool, or a combination of these and other natural materials which are capable of absorbing moisture and allowing air to permeate through to facilitate evaporation. The weight and thickness of the materials should be only the minimum necessary to keep the body comfortable and warm in cold weather while allowing the maximum access of air and sun during the warmer months.

It is axiomatic that the more we coddle our bodies the less efficient will our heating and cooling mechanisms become and the greater our liability to suffer the miseries arising when circumstances expose us to chilling or over-heating. Indeed, it is the sudden heat-loss which occurs when a hot, clammy body is suddenly cooled that triggers off so many of the so-called 'summer colds' – subject, of course, to the pre-existence of a somewhat run-down condition of general health.

A similar chain of circumstances arises when one induces heavy perspiration by soaking in a hot bath and then moves into a much cooler or draughty room. This is another example of the many ways in which man differs from the lesser orders, inasmuch as he is the only creature which deliberately exposes his body to abnormally high temperatures – externally by immersing himself in hot water, and internally by consuming very hot foods and beverages.

Anyone who has kept a dog as a pet will know that even the tastiest food will be shunned if it is served hot, and considerable resistance will be aroused by any attempt to subject the animal to even a moderately hot bath.

There are two clear lessons here for humans if we will only consider the implications. Most of us know from experience that heat is capable of softening even the toughest animal and vegetable materials, which of course is the principle which we employ in cooking to make otherwise inedible foods acceptable to the palate. Similarly, hot water is a very much more efficient solvent than a cold liquid.

It follows, therefore, that when we repeatedly take very hot food into the mouth it will have a softening effect on the mucous membranes of the tongue, palate and throat and disrupt the functions of the congested and inflamed salivary glands. Hot beverages such as soup, tea or coffee may be even more harmful inasmuch as they dissolve and flush away the protective mucus.

By the same token, washing in hot water, and especially soaking the body daily in a hot bath, softens the tissues, causes congestion in the superficial blood-vessels and removes the natural oily secretions which protect the skin from harmful bacteria, keep it supple and healthy, and filter out harmful radiation when our bodies are exposed to the sun.

These are considerations which need to be borne in mind by all health-seekers, including of course those who suffer from any catarrhal malady, inasmuch as they explain why we stress the importance of including in a whole-food diet raw fruits, vegetables and salads and cold drinks.

They justify, also, the recommendation that only cool or cold water shall be used for washing purposes and that a cool or cold sponge-down or shower should be taken daily, followed by a brisk friction-rub with a skin-brush or very coarse towel, not only to strengthen the body's first line of defence and stimulate the circulation, but also to reactivate the natural 'thermostats' which, when encouraged to do so, can stabilize the body temperature with remarkable efficiency and make us impervious to all but the most extreme and sudden climatic changes.

A moderately hot bath may be taken once weekly, but this should be followed by the sponge-down and friction rub.

Finally, we must mention briefly the very great importance of relaxation and adequate sleep and the need to minimize physical and emotional stress as far as possible.

Ill health is undoubtedly a major cause of anxiety, but because it is equally true that worry is at least partially responsible for a great deal of ill-health – both mental and physical – the two can frequently constitute a vicious circle in which they tend to perpetuate each other.

In the context of any metabolic illness, including catarrh, it needs to be understood that mental or emotional stress inhibits the functions of the digestive and assimilative organs and so undermines the body's vitality and recuperative powers. While we recognize that there is no simple formula which can be employed to safeguard us against the day-to-day stresses arising from domestic and occupational problems, there is no justification for nurturing negative and destructive anxieties concerning our health problems once we recognize that they are largely self-inflicted through ignorance of their true nature and causes, and that, by the same token, they are capable of resolution when positive steps are taken to release and mobilize the body's tremendous capacity for self-healing.

It is to this end that we shall now set out in simple terms a practical programme incorporating the various natural treatment procedures which we have discussed in detail in the preceding chapters and on which, it is hoped, the reader is now ready to embark with confidence based on knowledge and understanding.

10.

Self-treatment
Schedule

The initial spring-cleaning regime which we outlined in Chapter 8 can be commenced at any time of the year, but whenever possible it is advisable to choose a period when, for the first three or four days at least, and preferably for a week, it is possible to rest and relax as much as possible and be relatively free from social and occupational commitments.

For many people, this can be achieved by initiating treatment on a Friday and continuing over the week-end, or by taking a few days' holiday, and the housewife or mother may be able to enlist the co-operation of her spouse or another relative in order to minimize the demands on her time.

It is recognized that personal circumstances will dictate the extent to which readers are able to adhere to the suggested programmes, and it is permissible, therefore, to make minor adjustments to the sequence and timing of the various treatment measures provided that they are carried out within the daily schedule and that the dietary restrictions are strictly adhered to. It is in order, therefore, to interchange midday and evening meals, but not to make significant changes in their components.

Also, although every effort should be made to undertake an outdoor exercise session at least once and preferably twice daily, it can be fitted into the daily routine at any time that is convenient. The same applies to the breathing exercises, the purpose of which is to clear stagnant residual air from the deeper recesses of the lungs and improve the mobility of the rib-cage.

Appendix B on page 116 gives details of a number of useful auxiliary techniques which may be incorporated into the basic treatment schedule at the reader's discretion. They are intended to be used mainly to relieve any localized symptoms which may arise from time to time as part of the tissue-cleansing activities.

It should be remembered that the process of clearing the tissues of deep-seated catarrhal congestion cannot be accomplished in a few weeks, and that the eliminative reactions in the form of colds, sore throat, etc. may recur from time to time, though with decreasing frequency as the treatment measures become increasingly effective.

The occurrence of one of these 'healing crises', as they are rightly termed, should be the cue for putting into effect the following 'spring-cleaning' regime.

Here, then, is a summary of the day-to-day therapeutic programme which needs to be carried out in order to mobilize the body's self-healing faculties and cleanse it of the toxic residues which have over-burdened the mucous membranes and diverted them from their normal protective functions.

Self-Cleansing Programme

First three days

1. *Immediately on rising* each morning take a tumbler of one of the proprietary mineral waters – e.g. Malvern, Perrier, Evian, etc. Alternatively, if mineral water cannot be obtained, dissolve a level teaspoon of Epsom salts or Glauber's salts in a tumbler of warm water.
2. *Deep-breathing exercises* (see Appendix A on page 114) preferably in open air or a well-ventilated room.
3. *Sponge-down* the whole body, using a large face-flannel or small hand-towel wrung out in cold water, then dry briskly with a coarse towel, followed by a friction-rub with a skin brush or bath brush, if available.
4. *Breakfast:* Up to 300g (12 oz) of any *one* kind of fresh fruit – e.g. apples, pears, oranges, grapefruit, etc., but not bananas, and half a

tumbler of fresh or bottled unsweetened fruit juice diluted with an equal quantity of water.

5. *Brisk walk* or other outdoor exercise if possible, combined with deep-breathing.

6. *Midday:* As for breakfast, or a bowl of vegetable soup may replace fruit juice if preferred (see recipe in Appendix D, page 119).

7. *Early evening:* Outdoor exercise if convenient, or take later in evening if preferred.

8. *Evening meal:* As for midday.

9. *Before retiring:* Breathing exercises, followed by sponge-down and friction rub. Retire early in a well-ventilated bedroom. If a window cannot be left partially open, the door should be left ajar.

Notes:

Only *one* variety of fruit should be taken at each meal. During the day, drinks of water or dilute fruit juice may be taken, but only when needed to satisfy thirst. No other foods or beverages of any kind may be taken.

Normal activities may be continued as necessary, but anything involving undue physical or mental strain should be avoided as far as possible.

Those who are overweight or who are suffering from a chronic catarrhal ailment may well extend this part of the cleansing regime to four or five days.

Next four days

1. *On rising* take the juice of an orange or half a lemon in a glass of water, sweetened if desired with a teaspoon of honey. No other sweetener may be taken.
2. *Breathing exercises*, followed by sponge-down and friction-rub.
3. *Breakfast:* Fruit only as on preceding days.
4. *Outdoor exercise* if possible.
5. *Midday:* Bowl of vegetable soup (recipe in Appendix D, page 119).
6. *Early evening (or later):* Outdoor exercise.
7. *Evening meal:* Raw salad – e.g. lettuce, tomato, watercress; diced or sliced carrot or apple, with two steamed green or root vegetables (except potatoes).
8. *Before retiring:* Breathing exercises followed by sponge-down and friction-rub.

Notes:
During the early stages of the cleansing regime the eliminative organs are likely to be increasingly active, clearing the system of accumulated toxins. As a result, headache, furred tongue and other symptoms may be induced, causing a feeling of general malaise. This will usually clear in the course of a week or so, during which time it is desirable to rest as much as possible during the day in a darkened room. Take an Epsom salts bath (see Appendix C, page 118) on the first night before retiring

early, and repeat after four days until symptoms clear.

If there is no natural bowel movement *during any three-day period* of the cleansing programme a mild herbal laxative (obtainable from health food stores) may be taken.

Next seven days
As for preceding days except:

1. *Breakfast:* The same quantity of fruit, but mixed varieties may be taken if desired.
2. *Midday:* Raw salad as for previous evening meal, together with one or two slices of wholewheat bread or toast or crispbread spread thinly with low-fat margarine.
3. *Evening meal:* Bowl of vegetable soup, two or three steamed vegetables (except potato), and one or two items of fresh fruit.

Next seven days
As for preceding days except:

1. *Midday:* Small mixed salad with toast or crispbread or a baked jacket potato.
2. *Evening meal:* Two or three steamed vegetables with a little meat or fish, or an egg or cheese dish. Fresh fruit salad.

Notes:
The natural roughage in the diet, combined with the outdoor exercise, should ensure normal bowel function and so, provided that there has

been no tendency to over-eat and that the food has been eaten slowly and masticated thoroughly, it should be possible to dispense with the herbal laxative. Any slight sluggishness which may be experienced need cause no anxiety, as peristaltic rhythm will soon develop provided that there is no interference.

The cleansing programme is now completed and it is time to consolidate the benefits which have been achieved, bearing in mind, however, that further 'spring-cleaning' sessions may be needed from time to time – at intervals of two months or so – in order to fully restore systemic equilibrium and allow the mucous membranes to resume their normal functions.

In the meantime, it will be necessary to continue with the outdoor exercise and deep-breathing and the bathing procedures which play such an important part in maintaining heart, lung and circulatory efficiency.

Now, also, it becomes necessary to face up to the task of establishing new dietetic disciplines – of re-educating the palate to accept new tastes and textures and re-tooling the digestive 'chemical laboratories' in readiness for their new assimilative tasks.

The specimen menus set out in Appendix D on page 119 will serve as a guide to the type of meals which conform to the 20:20:60 formula which was explained in Chapter 8 (page 92), but the reader would be well advised to select a good wholefood cookery manual from the excellent range listed in the catalogue available from the publishers of this book, a selection of which is usually to be found on the shelves of most health food stores.

Newcomers to wholefood catering will, we think, be very agreeably surprised at the variety of wholesome and very appetizing meals which have been devised by the authors of these works, and which are gaining a rapidly expanding following among discerning and health-conscious members of the public, particularly the younger age-groups.

The latter are not only becoming increasingly health- and diet-conscious, but have also been largely responsible for the very widespread adoption of vegetarian principles, motivated partly by humanitarian considerations but also by the realization that animal proteins are not now regarded either as an essential or even a desirable component of the human diet. Indeed, there is a growing acceptance of the view that an excessive consumption of meat and animal fats is an important contributory factor in certain serious degenerative diseases, including kidney failure, high blood-pressure and coronary heart-disease.

While naturopaths do not all advocate a vegetarian diet as being essential to health, they are almost unanimous in insisting that animal proteins and fats should be eaten only in the strictest moderation as part of a balanced, wholefood diet.

The non-vegetarian reader should, therefore, keep these points very carefully in mind, and perhaps either purchase or borrow from a public library a good vegetarian wholefood cookery book as a preliminary to reaching a decision on what is, perhaps, still a rather controversial subject.

In conclusion, all sufferers from catarrhal ailments are urged to re-read all that has been written in the preceding chapters of this book in order that they may fully appreciate that their health problems cannot be 'cured' by any external agency, and that lasting relief from their symptoms and immunity from future 'infection' must be achieved by their own efforts and their determination to restore the metabolic and biochemic balance which alone can maintain 'wholeness' or health.

APPENDIX A:

Breathing Exercises

It is recommended that the following breathing exercises should be practised at least once daily, but preferably twice – either on rising and before retiring, or at any other convenient times.

Each movement should be repeated from six to twelve times, depending upon physical capacity.

1. Stand erect with head held high, feet astride and hands pressing lightly on the abdomen with finger-tips touching and thumbs just under the lower ribs.

   Breathe in, through the nose if possible, slowly and deeply, feeling the ribs rising and the abdomen protruding slightly as the diaphragm contracts.

   Breathe out slowly, allowing the ribs to lower and pulling in the abdomen as strongly as possible.

2. Standing erect as for first exercise and still with head high, but with the arms at sides, breathe out as fully as possible, then, while breathing , circle the arm slowly forwards upwards, sideways and downwards three or four times, then breathe out, slowly, continuing to circle the arms.

Rest for a few seconds, breathing normally, then repeat.

3. To reduce tension in the neck and stimulate circulation to the head, stand or sit erect, with arms folded and chin on chest. Without allowing the shoulders to move, turn the head to the right, then raise it as high as possible, turn it to the left, then lower and return to starting position so that the chin describes as wide a circle as possible.

Relax for a few moments, then repeat in the opposite direction.

Note:
The range of movement in exercises 2 and 3 may be somewhat limited at first and care should be taken to avoid undue strain. Creaking and crackling noises may be heard, but they should tend to diminish gradually and eventually cease as joint-mobility is gradually improved.

APPENDIX B:

Local Relief Measures

The following techniques may be employed from time to time, as necessary, to relieve local congestion and inflammation.

1. Nose-breathing is often restricted by narrowing of the nostrils and swelling of the mucous linings. Gradual improvement may be effected by:

   (a) Bending the head over a bowl of cold water, cupping a little in the palm of the hand, raising it to the nose and alternately sniffing gently and then blowing out, repeating for several minutes.

   (b) Bending the head over a bowl of boiling water, covering the head with a towel and inhaling the steam alternately through the nose and mouth, raising or lowering the head as necessary to control the heat within comfortable limits. Continue for ten to fifteen minutes, then apply a cloth or small towel, wrung out in cold water, to the eyes, nose and mouth for a minute or two.

(c) Inserting the first joint of the little finger into each nostril in turn and moving it in circles, mobilizing the bony central septum and stretching the walls of the nostrils.

(d) Frequently, throughout the day, consciously flaring the nostrils as widely as possible while inhaling, then relaxing while exhaling.

(e) To relieve throat soreness and hoarseness, gargle with a glass of cold water to which has been added two teaspoons of lemon juice.

APPENDIX C:

Epsom Salts Bath

In the event of an acute flare-up in the form of a cold, influenza, tonsillitis, etc., the full three-weeks' cleansing regime should be carried out. To promote perspiration and so encourage maximum eliminative activity via the skin, dissolve three pounds of commercial Epsom salts in a bath of hot water and remain immersed for from ten to twenty minutes, during which time a flannel wrung out repeatedly in cold water should be applied to the forehead.

Retire to bed immediately, with a hot-water bottle at the feet, taking care to avoid chilling.

On rising, take a cool or cold sponge-down and friction-rub.

Repeat after four days if symptoms persist.

Note:
Commercial Epsom salts may be obtained from most chemists, usually in 3kg (7lb) packs.

APPENDIX D:

Specimen Menus and Recipes

Breakfast

(a) Fresh fruit – two or three items of any variety – e.g. apple, orange, pear, ½ grapefruit – with ¼ pint natural yogurt.

(b) Stewed or soaked dried fruit – e.g. prunes, apricots, figs, raisins, sultanas.

(c) Muesli (see recipe on page 122).

(d) Once or twice a week *only*: wholegrain cereal moistened with two or three dessertspoons of skimmed milk and water. If sweetening is desired, dissolve a little honey in the liquid.

Midday

(a) Small mixed salad. Select 3 or 4 from lettuce, tomato, cucumber, watercress and diced or sliced raw carrot or beetroot, with one slice wholewheat bread or toast or crispbread, spread with low-fat margarine and yeast extract or peanut butter.

(b) Two or three slices of wholewheat bread or

toast or crispbread with a poached or scrambled egg or 50g (2 oz) cheese, and an apple or banana.
(c) Two steamed vegetables with 50g (2 oz) lean meat or fish, or a vegetarian savoury.

Evening
(a) Large mixed salad (see recipe on page 122) with two slices of wholewheat bread or toast or crispbread spread with peanut butter or honey, followed by stewed fresh or dried fruit sprinkled with a dessertspoon of wheat-germ.
(b) A mixed vegetable casserole sprinkled with 50g (2 oz) of grated cheese, followed by fresh fruit salad and $\frac{1}{4}$ pint natural yogurt.
(c) Two steamed green or root vegetables, with 50g (2 oz) lean meat or fish and a baked jacket potato, followed by a baked apple stuffed with sultanas or dates.
(d) An omelette or vegetarian savoury with salad or steamed vegetables, followed by sliced banana in natural yogurt, or fresh fruit.

Notes:
1. Select meals to ensure that a salad and some fresh fruit is taken each day.
2. Do not chop or grate vegetables or fruits as this causes maximum destruction of vitamins. They should be diced or sliced and then served immediately. Lettuce and other green vegetables should be torn into pieces if necessary.
3. Proprietary salad dressings, salt, pickles and

other condiments should not be added to food either at the table or during cooking. If a salad dressing is desired it should consist of natural yogurt or a dessertspoon of olive oil or corn oil mixed with a teaspoon of lemon juice. A little celery salt may be added to vegetables if desired.

4. Drinks should be taken only between meals and should consist preferably of water, or diluted fruit or vegetable juices, or half a teaspoon of yeast extract in warm water. A cup of unsweetened tea or decaffeinated coffee may be taken occasionally if desired.

5. Fruit and vegetables should be washed or scrubbed thoroughly, but should remain unpeeled if possible.

Recipes

Clear Vegetable Soup
Prepare approximately 2kg (4½ lb) of any vegetables – e.g. cabbage, carrots, celery, onions, spinach, tomatoes, parsley, peas and beans – diced or sliced as necessary, cover with 1¼ litres (2 pints) boiling water and simmer for 1 hour. Strain and flavour with yeast extract, but do not add salt or other condiments.

Muesli
Proprietary muesli cereals are now very widely available, but many of them contain sugar and are expensive.

A cheaper and very nutritious alternative can be made up from the following ingredients to provide a very satisfying breakfast dish or a light midday or evening meal.

2 or 3 heaped dessertspoons coarse oatmeal
1 level dessertspoon honey (optional)
1 heaped dessertspoon washed raisins, sultanas or chopped dates
2 heaped dessertspoons grated nuts (peanuts, hazels, cashews, etc.)
½ medium apple
½ ripe banana
4 dessertspoons warm water (or half skimmed milk and water)

Mix the dried fruit into the oatmeal, melt the honey (if desired) in the warm water, pour over the oatmeal and leave to soak for one hour or overnight.

Before serving add the finely chopped apple, sprinkle over the grated nuts and decorate with banana slices.

Mixed Salad

Lettuce, tomato, carrot, beetroot (raw or cooked, but no vinegar), cucumber, celery, watercress, etc. as available.*

1 dessertspoon washed dried fruit (raisins, sultanas, dates, etc.)
50g (2 oz) cheese

* The basic salad ingredients may be varied as necessary according to season.

50g (2 oz) grated nuts (peanuts, hazels, cashews, etc.)
½ medium apple
½ ripe banana

Tear the lettuce into pieces and line a large plate, then decorate with sliced tomato, cucumber, diced carrot, etc.

Dice the apple finely and scatter over, followed by the dried fruit, then grate the cheese and sprinkle over, followed by the grated nuts, and decorate with sliced banana.

Index